To Mike Palko,
Congratulations on
your great walks!
Best wishes!
Bob Sweetgall

# THE WALKER'S JOURNAL

ROBERT SWEETGALL
JOHN DIGNAM

## EXPERIENCING AMERICA ON FOOT

Published by:
CREATIVE WALKING, INC.
175 Elkton Road
Newark, DE 19711

Copyright © 1986
Robert Sweetgall, John Dignam
ISBN 0–939041–02–2

*Other books by Robert Sweetgall*

Fitness Walking
Walking Wellness—A Student Workbook
Walking Wellness—Teacher's Curriculum Guidebook

*Special Credits*

Artwork and layout: John Carlisle, Jane Nieland and Lynn Burds of Carlisle Graphics.

The 52 weekly stories on Robert Sweetgall's walk originally appeared in The Evening Gazette and are reprinted with the permission of The Worcester Telegram & Gazette.

*Special Acknowledgements*

To the Worcester Telegram & Gazette (T&G) and its publisher and editor, Robert C. Achorn and Kenneth J. Botty respectively. . . to Diane Benison, managing editor of The (Worcester) Evening Gazette . . . to Daniel Sullivan, Betty Lewis and the T&G Promotion Department . . . to the research teams at the University of Massachusetts Medical Center and the University of Massachusetts Departments of Exercise Science and Human Nutrition . . . to the Dupont Biomedical Products Department . . . to Lyons Studios . . . and to the corporate sponsors of this 50-state walk: W. L. Gore & Associates (Fabrics Div.) and The Rockport (Shoe) Company.

Printed in the United States of America
    4 5 6 7 8 9 10

**The Cover**    Rob Sweetgall: Walking the Mojave Desert.
Cover design: Lynne Tesch . . . Photograph: Eric Crossan.

To my best teachers: my parents, Sylvia and Murray, and Dr. Robert E. Neeves . . . and to the hundreds of trusting Americans who helped me on the road.

—RJS—

To my family.

—JD—

# Introduction

It would seem a simple thing to sum up Rob Sweetgall's walk around the United States. This man took a walk to deliver a message. The walk was 11,208 miles. The message was: Take care of your health.

That message was both his purpose and his accomplishment.

But between the first step and the last was a marvelous adventure of long, lonely days and friendly encounters, spectacular scenery, icy winds and brutal heat, eager school children, public indifference and enthusiasm, successes, disappointments, individual kindnesses and sharing.

And always, as backdrop, there was the beauty, silence, noise, diversity emptiness and crowds that is the United States. 11,208 miles. Twenty million footsteps, 3 pairs of shoes. Thousands of people, cities and towns, 364 days, 24 blisters.

For Rob, the romance of the walk was secondary to his message of health and was often clouded by the unbending push to keep to schedule. But to many who followed it in weekly stories in The (Worcester, Mass.) Evening Gazette, there was the romance of the road. For many of us, Rob was taking the walk we always had wanted to take, and he was taking us with him.

The Gazette's coverage of the walk came after I wrote a story on his planned journey. I had been working on a story at the University of Massachusetts Medical Center when someone said a man was undergoing testing there before walking around the country. After that story, Rob suggested it might be a nice idea if he called us once in a while from the road so readers would know how his walk was going. The editors decided to run a week-by-week update.

Each week Rob would call me and describe where he was and what had happened during the past week. His calls came at midnight on Wednesdays, and 5 a.m. on Thursdays. They came from restaurants and homes, bars and gasoline stations, from phone booths in

Photo by Harry Dorshaw.

**Calling Collect from the Road**   Fifty-two times during his walk, Robert Sweetgall was interviewed on the phone by John Dignam for the stories that ran weekly in The Evening Gazette. The calls lasted at least an hour.

crowded lobbies or on empty highways. In the background might be a whoosh of a tractor trailer, the lowing of a cow or the music of a jukebox.

The stuff of adventure—the uncertainty of what was ahead, where he would sleep, how he would find food, what weather would he meet, what dangers did traffic pose. It was history in the making.

I would be sitting at my desk at 5:30 a.m., the office warm, the coffee steaming, my eyes barely open. But when Rob called and described the wind freezing the waves on a lake or the cars fighting him for space on a narrow road, I woke up.

Rob is a sharp-eyed, attentive observer and what he experienced, readers experienced—the expanse of Montana, the boredom and heat of Nebraska, Alabama fire ants, the elation and depression.

When the walk started there seemed to be little interest. But as 500 miles turned into 2,000 miles and 4,000 miles, as people realized this man was out there *alone* with only a four-pound waist pack, interest grew. People in coffee shops and children in schools talked about "the walker." On Thursdays, newspapers in the Gazette city room were opened to that week's Sweetgall story.

When Rob made a brief appearance in Worcester near the end of the walk, 1,000 people turned out to hear him.

To me, the surprise of this adventure was that Rob Sweetgall at the end of the trek was much like Sweetgall at the beginning—mildly amused by his reputation as a "serious walker," but adamant on the subject of health.

Privately, he is a quiet, almost shy person. Publicly, he is an articulate, forceful advocate of fitness and health. He has remained convinced that Americans should be made aware that they can and should do more for their health, to cut down on the risk factors that cause heart disease, to walk for exercise.

The stories reprinted here are the stories that followed Rob Sweetgall around the United States—from his first footstep to the day he finished his walk in New York City amid banners, bands and hundreds of people, so unlike most days of his walk. But the "updates" of Rob's walk are more than just newspaper stories, they are the saga of a truly daring journey.

*John Dignan*

# Motivation

My life story is simple: Brooklyn boy, an only child liking math and science, grows up to be a chemical engineer. He works 12 years for DuPont and suddenly quits at age 33 to trek across America. He completes his mission, preaching on cardiovascular health, and decides to do it again. On his second trek, he promotes walking by walking. All 50 states. Within that next year—September '84 to September '85—he walks 11,208 miles.

QUESTION: How did that shy, flabby Flatbush boy nicknamed "Butterball" by his cousins and "Sweet Gal" by his classmates, get from sidewalk stickball to highway hiking and stripping naked in public laundromats to wash his road clothes? The stripping part was easy. I just asked housewives to turn their heads. The highway walking wasn't difficult either. Slow and steady gets you there. A step at a time. The tough part is taking that first step—walking away from your career.

Lifestyle. I joined DuPont in 1969 as a 198 pound deconditioned academian raring to design chemical plants. By 1981 I was a 165 pound triathlete—marathoner, punching raw material prices into a computer terminal and taking 1½ hour lunches to swim-run-walk at the "Y."

From 1969 to 1981 I had witnessed enough family grave sites to realize the value of health. By luck in 1972, I heard Professor Robert Neeves speak on cardiovascular risk factors at a DuPont safety meeting. Talk about dynamicism. He flashed color slides of cholesterol deposits in arteries of high-fat eaters and smokers who rarely exercised. Lifestyle, indeed.

After Neeves' talk, my training skyrocketed into fitness fanaticism. In 1981 I quit my $50,000 DuPont job. I was a bachelor, willing to shovel rocks anytime I needed to put food on the table. I just wanted to be a full-time health-fitness something. A new career, yet to be defined. How many times had I listened to my colleagues talk about their dreams, daring themselves to leave behind their corporate nest egg and embryonic pension. Security.

I figured it this way; if I had my health, I had everything. If I could achieve one thing in life I was proud of—something that benefitted others and my health too—then what more could I ask for? With this rationale, I kept idealizing. Finally a plan jelled in my mind. In 1981 I founded a public charity, The Foundation for the Development of Cardiovascular Health, and through it organized a school health lecture tour—on foot—to trek America's perimeter talking at schools en route. If I could be half the speaker Dr. Neeves was, what impact I could have on young children. So it started. Physical training, project planning, mapping the route, fund raising (thank you Gore-Tex and Rockport), writing letters to schools, learning to speak, and getting it all together for 10,000 miles on the road. A start—1982.

I have done it twice now—a 10,608 mile walk-run (mostly walking thank God) in 1982–83 and an 11,208 miler (pure walking) in 1984–85. I have no regrets. Sometimes I wondered what I was doing out there—limping on hot blisters in the desert, sloshing through spring blizzards. It's no picnic. The days are long, the work often tense. The "job" pays about 3¢ an hour (coins found on the road), and you beg a lot of favors. The rewards are the experiences—meeting new people, discovering America, discovering yourself.

People have called me crazy. Others have told me that I'm wasting my time. Some view me as a fanatic trying to build an army of health nuts. But I'm not. My message isn't that you should quit your job to walk across America. Nor is it that you need to walk 31 miles a day as I did to stay healthy. My point is that in our society we overemphasize the material side of life—new cars, color TVs, big homes. Yet these are all replaceable objects. The one thing we own that is irreplaceable is our health. Often that's what we neglect the most.

Where does walking fit in? By simply stepping out each day, a mile here and a mile there, we can improve our chances for lifelong wellness—and for free. The great thing about walking is that we need not be athletes to do it. In our own way, we can all walk this country of ours.

So picture the two of us sitting in front of your livingroom TV, munching chocolate chippers, sloshing sodas. I say to you, let's get healthy. You nod back. I make a motion to rise. We do. You kill the TV and together we head to the front door. You open it. A soft breeze brushes your hair back, cooling your face and scalp. Outside white clouds sail the blue sky. Down the block we head, passing lawns and flowers and trees you never knew your neighbors owned. Heel-toe. Right-left. Heel-toe. Right-left. Our eyes are opening, our minds awakening, our bodies energizing. After ten minutes we look back. Your house is out of sight. Westward we continue, heading for the church steeple that now kisses the sun. I point to the water tower ahead, the next town, 2 miles away.

"Should we go for it?," I ask. "What do you say?"

"Piece of cake," you answer with a confident smile. You're getting that vagabond spirit.

There you go. You're on your way across America.

*Robert Sweetgall*

# Using Your Journal

Using the 3 log-charts below, you can walk (and plot) your way through 50 states this year. You will *not* need to walk 31 miles per day to do it either. By walking 20 to 25 miles per week—as recommended by many medical scientists today—you can improve your chances of enjoying lifelong wellness while discovering America too.

Remember, for every ONE mile you walk, you receive credit for TEN. That way you can walk from Marmarth, ND across Montana to Spokane, WA (almost 900 miles) in just four weeks. And there are some great guest houses to sleep in along the way.

# The A, B, C's of Walking America

## STEP A

Start on any given Saturday: Log your daily mileage. Come Friday, calculate your weekly total.
NOTE: You can start your log at any time of the year.

## STEP B

Every other Friday: Record your 2-week mileage total (column B) and calculate your cumulative mileage (column C). Multiply your cumulative mileage by 10 to find your adjusted mileage (column E).

## STEP C

Match your adjusted mileage to the mileages shown on pages 112–114 to find out where you'll be sleeping Friday night.

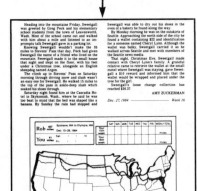

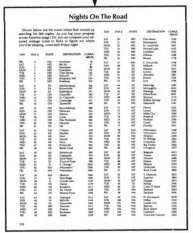

## EXAMPLE

Winnie and Walter Walker are walking across America together. Each night after dinner they go out strolling in their neighborhood to knock off a stretch of transcontinental highway. Most often they cover 2 miles. On weekends they are putting in extra time to maintain their 22 mile per week pace. Currently they are finishing their 8th week. Winnie and Walter have each tallied 172 miles for an *adjusted mileage total 1720,* which puts them in Benson, Minnesota on schedule on Friday night, the 56th day of the journey. That earns them a "good" nights sleep on the hardwood floor of a grain elevator (Rob's mattress that 56th night). But Winnie and Walter will not have to worry. Their grain elevator shack is heated, and there are stacks of 25-pound dog food bags that make excellent pillows.

You are now ready to begin
your walk across America.

# Table of Contents

# Appalachia

**Starting an 11,208 Mile Walk**
Over 150 6th-graders from
Mote Elementary School
started this 50-state journey
with me. They all walked 3.5
miles into Maryland. Many
expressed concern for my
getting hurt. Others wanted to
know where I'd sleep that
night, and if my legs were
getting tired already.

Photo by DuPont Magazine.

# Blue Highways, Red Feet

MARYLAND — Route 40 and heading west.

Robert J. Sweetgall finished the day yesterday with blisters on his feet and concern about Hurricane Diana, two things he did not anticipate when he started his around-the-country walk last Friday. But, he said, both have been offset by the warm reception of people along the route.

"The storm's moving north at about 10 miles an hour. I'm going west at about 4 miles an hour," Sweetgall said in a telephone interview yesterday. "Maybe it won't catch me."

While the possibility of flooded roads due to the hurricane concerned him yesterday, his main worry was a blister the size of a marble which he discovered Saturday, when he awakened.

"Because I wasn't in shape, starting the walk was like telling a pole vaulter to put out a maximum performance without a running start." He said he is overweight, out of shape, carrying about eight pounds of equipment and walking his 30,000 steps a day in unseasonably warm weather.

"My feet are really taking a beating, but it'll straighten out. I walk on the grass where ever I can," he said. He said he was very surprised to get such a blister this early into the walk, "but there are no major problems."

He said he is walking a little less than four miles per hour for about 12 hours a day and stopping every hour to air his foot to promote the blister's healing and avoid infection. He's getting about five hours sleep a night. He has walked 152 miles.

"It'll probably take a few weeks to a month to get into shape," said Sweetgall. Then he will increase his pace and decrease walking to about eight hours a day.

Yesterday, he walked west on Route 40 through the hilly countryside with temperatures in the mid-80s. He expected to find a place to stay tonight in Flintstone, Md., "a town of no motels and about 500 people in the mountains" and was heading for Cumberland, Md., today.

Sweetgall has arranged to address assemblies of students at different communities along the way.

At the start of the walk, principal Paul Carlson told the 150 sixth-graders at the Anne P. Mote School in Newark, Del., that they could walk the 3.5 miles to the Maryland line. They all made it.

At Clear Springs, he was met by a 9-year-old girl who watched him tend his blister at a service station. "We started talking about what I was doing and she asked if I would speak at her school," he said. "It was finally arranged at a hurried midnight phone call to the school principal and I spoke there today (yesterday)."

While some lodging is prearranged, some is not. He walked into the volunteer fire department in Hampstead, Md., (population 500) Sunday and asked where he could find a place to stay. They directed him to the home of Mayor Julia Gouge, who apologized for the leftover vegetables at supper and put him up in a motor coach in the back yard.

To help pass time, Sweetgall said he keeps a running tab of all the money he finds along the road. After five days he has $1.10, mostly pennies.

*Sept. 13, 1984 ——————————— Week 1*

TRIADELPHIA, W. Va. — The breakfast special was 99 cents, coffee 25 cents extra. Jars of pigs feet were lined up above the beer cooler and country music played loudly in the background.

Robert J. Sweetgall walked into Brownie's Pub and Restaurant late yesterday morning after speaking to about 1,000 students in two schools in nearby Washinton, Pa., a community of about 50,000.

He would be in his third state of the day later, after he walked through Wheeling, W.Va., and looked for a place to stay in the small towns of Brookside or Lansing, Ohio.

Sweetgall said that despite a minor sore throat he feels the best he has since beginning his walk Sept. 7 in his hometown of Newark, Del. His blisters are healing and his body is toughening up, he said.

Sweetgall said he missed hurricane Diana last week, getting only a couple of hours of rain Saturday morning in Frostburg, Pa.

"Very blue skies. It's getting more like autumn, 65 to 70 degrees. It makes it easier to walk," Sweetgall said.

"I'm about done with the mountains, and I think it will be flatter and easier from here on."

Sweetgall said he has been walking 28 to 29 miles a day. He is putting in 14-hour days, including his stops at schools to talk with students about health and exercise.

He generally stays in homes or motels, although twice in the past week he has been hard pressed to find a place to stay. He said he became stuck in the mountains last Wednesday when he passed through Flintstone, Md., and hoped to make Cumberland by nightfall. He said he stopped at an auction in the mountains for about an hour and ended walking up the mountain in the dark.

His foot very sore from blisters, he began walking down nine miles of steep, narrow mountain road in the dark when he found the Stone Lodge. "An old woman let me stay for $16 and sold me a loaf of bread and cheese," he said. "Four or five Swiss cheese sandwiches were my supper and breakfast."

At Brownsville, Pa., a small town in the mountains that has been hard hit by the slumping steel industry, Sweetgall said the police station seemed the best bet for sleeping quarters until Jim Morriston let him sleep upstairs over his 24-hour restaurant. "He gave me a sleeping bag, a custard pie and tea for my sore throat," he said.

At Washington, Pa., Tuesday night Sweetgall stayed at the home of Rotary Club member Andy Uram. On the autograph covered walls of Uram's basement, Sweetgall signed his name next to Neil Bush, who had stopped there while campaigning for his father, Vice President George Bush, during presidential primaries four years ago.

To help pass time, Sweetgall said he keeps a running tab of all the money he finds along the road. As of yesterday morning, he had $4.44 — 39 cents per day in Pennsylvania, 33 cents per day in Maryland and nothing in Delaware or West Virginia. Included were two quarters he found on the road early one morning near a note students had left — "held down by a stake and four rocks" — thanking him for talking at their school the day before.

*Sept. 20, 1984* ——————————— *Week 2*

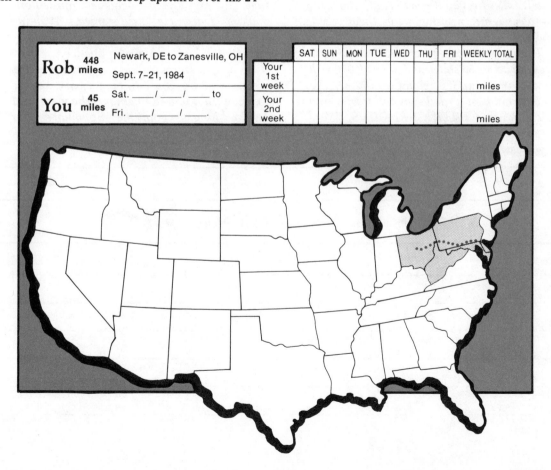

| | | SAT | SUN | MON | TUE | WED | THU | FRI | WEEKLY TOTAL |
|---|---|---|---|---|---|---|---|---|---|
| **Rob** 448 miles | Newark, DE to Zanesville, OH<br>Sept. 7–21, 1984 | Your 1st week | | | | | | | | miles |
| **You** 45 miles | Sat. ___/___/___ to<br>Fri. ___/___/___. | Your 2nd week | | | | | | | | miles |

### 1 · Starting Out

What's it like to start an 11,208-mile walk? For me it was a melting pot of emotions: Tension (opening day jitters), Sadness (saying good-by to family and friends), Worry (what did I forget to pack?), Excitement (what lies on the road ahead?), and Relief (at last, I'm on my way!).

When you "solo it" across America, life is by the moment—where you'll sleep, where you'll eat, who you'll meet. That's the fun of it—discovering new highways, new people, and yourself.

To many, it's incomprehensible how someone can cover 50 states and over 11,000 miles on foot in a year. It often hit me that way too as I'd walk past a road sign and turn around to check it out: BILLINGS 81 MILES. "Wow," I'd say to myself, "it seems as if I just left Billings yesterday." It makes you realize that little footsteps can add up to a lot. Slow, steady progress. As Abraham Lincoln said, "I am a slow walker, but I never walk backwards."

In 1861 Edward Payson Weston left Boston on foot to walk 453 miles to Washington, DC, in 10 days to attend Lincoln's inauguration. Weston trekked through snow, slush, and mud, arriving 10 hours late. Lincoln still came out and shook Weston's hand. From that day on, Weston achieved miraculous walking feats. He once wrote, "Walking would teach people the quality that youngsters find so hard to learn—patience."

So as you start "walking your way across America" in this journal, take it easy. Let the journey train you. Remember, the pavement lasts as long as your life. So what's your hurry? Enjoy the trip!

### 2 · Your Personal Foot Notes

# The Ohio Valley

Photo by John Lusk, Toledo Metroparks.

**The King of the Hoboes** You meet some unforgettable folks on a walk across America. Take Maurey "Steam Train" Graham, the man elected 5 times "King of the Hoboes" at the Hobo Convention in Britt, Iowa. "Steam Train" has a love for nature and the outdoors. He knows he can survive off the land anytime he needs to. For him, that is security.

# Walking the Old National Highway—Route 40 West

FOSTORIA, OHIO — President Reagan was the bigger attraction in this part of Ohio yesterday.

But that just made it more exciting for Rob Sweetgall.

"I was walking along and came up to a radio station — WFOB — that was right on the road, so I walked in to see if someone might want to do a quick interview. Well, Reagan was only about 30 miles away at Bowling Green (State University) and they had live reports coming in and there were media from all over the country there.

"They took the time to do a 10-minute tape with me. It was really exciting," Sweetgall said.

Sweetgall is about 590 miles into his walk through the United States. He's fighting the remnants of a cold and sore throat that he picked up last week, but his blisters have healed and his feet "are doing good."

He is averaging about 30 miles a day.

"But I have to cut down. I'm getting up too late and getting to bed too late, and I'm walking too long," he said in a telephone interview yesterday afternoon.

The weather has turned cool. Temperatures have dropped from the 80s to the 60s, he said. "That's been a big help, but I want it in the 30s and 40s. That's the best weather for me," he said.

Sweetgall has walked as many as 40 miles a day and as few as 25 miles a day this week.

"I now know I can do 40 miles in a day without discomfort, but I'm still not at the point I want. I could probably do two, 40-mile days, but I want to get it up to 50," he said.

"I'm not yet at four miles an hour. It will probably take me about a month to reach that."

Psychologically he's had a lot of "ups and downs" he said. "I think once I get a month under me I'll be okay. There's so much ahead, but at this point all I can do is look back and see what I've done already."

Sweetgall is into his second pair of shoes. "The brown leather ones, which we called Pair 11 for identification, did about 540 miles. They were still pretty good. I think they might have 300 or 400 miles left in them," he said.

Talking about the last week, he said it's been "a lot of motels, about six I think.

"And I've washed a lot of socks."

Sweetgall said he's been meeting a lot of interesting people along the way. He's stopped at a couple "drive-thrus," beverage markets which you can drive through and have beer and soda loaded right into your car.

He met an Ohio state trooper as he walked west in the eastbound lane of Interstate 70 in eastern Ohio.

"He pulled up on the median strip and I said to myself, 'Here we go'", Sweetgall said. Walking along interstates is illegal.

"We talked for about 10 minutes and finally he said, 'Basically, I didn't see you and you didn't see me. But if someone else sees you you could be arrested.'"

"I did my 10-mile stretch — there were no other roads to follow — and then I got off."

Sweetgall has been looking for change lying along the roads to help pass the time. "The college campus was a real rich stretch," he said. "I picked up a $1.38 that day."

The total since he left Newark, Del., stands at $7.81.

CHRISTINE R. DUNPHY

*Sept. 27, 1984* ————————— *Week 3*

HOWELL, Mich. — The land is getting flatter and where it isn't flat it rises gently into rolling hills.

Along the road are fields of corn or soybeans or herds of cattle, marked off by small farming communities of 1,000 to 5,000 people.

Robert J. Sweetgall is enjoying the walk. The wind is up, the temperature is down. "A little frost at night. It's good for the feet," Sweetgall said in a telephone interview yesterday. "Cold crisp air. Skies have been blue for three days."

"And of course, there's the Tigers. Everything out here is Detroit Tigers now."

He was calling from a farm equipment company on Grand River Road. "It's the only telephone between here and Webberville," he said.

Sweetgall said he is a few miles behind schedule, but he is not concerned. When he gets a little ahead he stops at a school to talk with the students. When he falls behind, he picks up the pace.

Late last week, he found himself ahead of schedule so he walked into the Scotch Ridge School at 1 p.m., told the principal who he was and what he was doing, and asked if he could address the students.

"At 1:30 we put on a program in the gymnasium for 150 children in kindergarten through grade 4. I ended up walking in the rain for 3½ hours to Toledo, but the stop was worth it. It really picked up my spirits."

He said he now is averaging about 29 miles per day, a little under the 32 miles per day he needs to finish the trip on schedule. But he said he is getting into good physical condition. He said, "I feel like I could do 40 if I have to."

In Howell, "I walked into a confectionary shop that was just about to close," he said. "It was like the old drugstores — the silver container that was put on the green mixer to make malteds."

The owner's daughter, a young high school girl, made him an orange canteloupe malted. "It wasn't on the menu, but she said it was very good. I guess that's the melon capital," he said. "Every year they have a melon festival. Anyway, that was supper, then I walked a mile to a Holiday Inn."

His favorite meal now is salads, often salad bars in fast food restaurants. He uses his one-third, one-half or one-cup yellow measuring cups to check amounts. (He is sending weekly reports on what he eats to the department of food science and nutrition at the University of Massachusetts, Amherst.)

A good-size meal consists of one-half cup servings of about six items, including cottage cheese, corn, green peas, chick peas, cole slaw, red beets, carrots, broccoli or potato salad. "The kale that they use for decoration I steal off the ice," he said, "and that's my green leaf vegetable.

He eats about seven meals a day and snacks on fruits. Breakfast is toast and, egg whites, or pancakes, or cereal. He said, "I've been eating a lot (two cups at a serving) of cereal."

His collection of money found along the side of the road has increased to $10.10, mostly pennies. He said he found a 1939 wheatear penny which he will keep. The rest he spends.

*Oct. 4, 1984* ———————————— *Week 4*

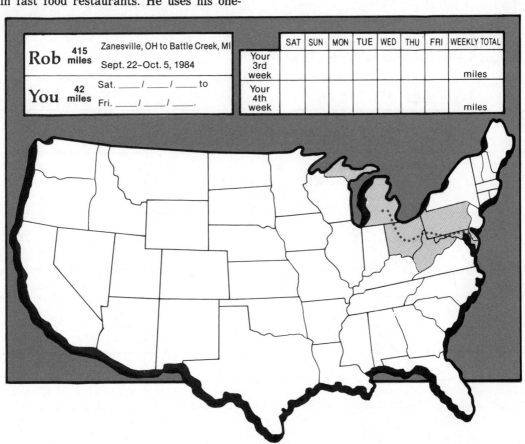

| Rob 415 miles | Zanesville, OH to Battle Creek, MI | | | SAT | SUN | MON | TUE | WED | THU | FRI | WEEKLY TOTAL |
|---|---|---|---|---|---|---|---|---|---|---|---|
| | Sept. 22–Oct. 5, 1984 | | Your 3rd week | | | | | | | | miles |
| You 42 miles | Sat. ___ / ___ / ___ to | | Your 4th week | | | | | | | | |
| | Fri. ___ / ___ / ___. | | | | | | | | | | miles |

---

**3**    A Tramp and a Hobo _____

    *I met the King of the Hoboes out at Toledo's Pearson Metropark. He was dressed in a shirt of red bandanna cloth and a Santa Claus beard. The King's walk was somewhat hunched, his weight largely supported on a twisted cane he once pulled out of the Louisiana bayous back in the days when he rode railroad boxcars. It didn't take long for this hobo named "Steam Train" to classify me:*

    *"You're a tramp. You didn't know that, did you?"*

    *"A tramp?," I begged his pardon.*

    *"I didn't mean to insult you, but a tramp is an honorable man. Yet the dictionary says he was a vagabond and stole to make his way. And that's a lie. Hoboes and tramps helped build this country. Helped build the railroads. And yet I heard people say to me, 'Did you steal a ride on that train?' And I'll answer back, 'No, I took a ride on that train!' You can't steal a ride on a train. The only way you can steal a ride is to take somebody else's seat. What are you stealing in an empty boxcar? Tramps never take rides though. They're purists at walking. Tramps have more pride than hoboes. No question about it, you're a tramp!"*

---

**4**    **Your Personal Foot Notes**

_____

_____

_____

_____

_____

_____

_____

_____

_____

# Dairyland

**The Human Guinea Pig** Eight times during the journey, I flew back to Boston to be tested at the University of Massachusetts so that scientists could learn more about the long-term effects of easy-gaited walking. Here I'm finishing a 2-hour treadmill stress test, walking up a 15% incline to determine cardiorespiratory adaptations.

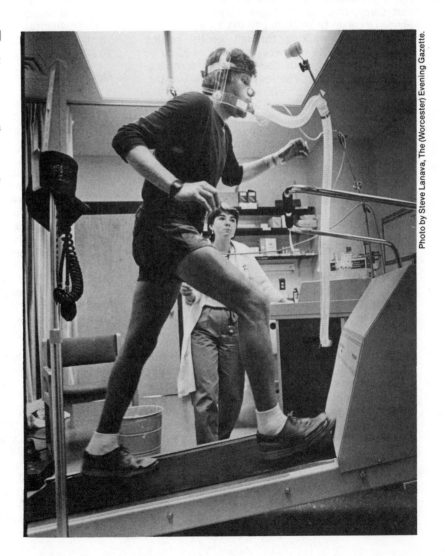

Photo by Steve Lanava, The (Worcester) Evening Gazette.

# After Chicago, It's Cheese Country

CHICAGO — This has been Rob Sweetgall's strongest week as far as mileage.

He has passed the 1,000-mile mark and has boosted his daily average to 35 miles, even putting in one 40-mile day. He said he is feeling strong and has not had a blister for 700 miles.

Yesterday, he said, was "a pure mileage day," with no stops planned. He started the day in the small town of Pines, Ind., where the passing trains had rattled the room of his small motel the night before. He walked through Hammond and Gary, Ind., to Michigan City, down Lake Shore Drive on Lake Michigan to Chicago.

He is still walking through gently rolling farmland, and the temperature daily is 50 to 60 degrees, warmer than the 30-degree temperature he would like. "The leaves are now turning, getting into reds and yellow," he said, "and the wind is whipping the leaves around."

He has traveled through small and large communities — from cities such as Lansing, Battle Creek and Kalamazoo to the towns such as Schoolcraft and Cassopolis.

"I spend a lot of time on foot care, about one-and-a-half hours per day, cooling them, massaging them, using moisturizing cream and powder," he said, "making sure I don't develop hot spots or blisters."

He has slept mostly in motels, although he spent one night sleeping over a truck stop in Pottersville, Mich.

Last Sunday he experienced his worst weather day. "It started to rain as I left the small motel in Schoolcraft, and it soon started raining harder. On the highway, it was your basic bullfrogs and nightcrawlers rain storm," he said.

After 37 miles he stopped at a restaurant in Vandalia where about 20 people were celebrating a birthday. "There was no motel and no offer for a place to stay," he said, "so I kept walking."

At Cassopolis, accountant Beth Baker was working late at her insurance company. She said she and her husband Pat would be glad to put Sweetgall up at their home in Dowagiac.

"They have pit bulls, which are dogs used in dog fighting, but the Bakers don't use the dogs for that," he said. Sweetgall spent the night near the dogs, "the nicest dogs. You couldn't imagine. They had four but Duchess attacked Max so they had to get rid of Duchess. Really friendly dogs, though," he said.

In a suburb of South Bend, Ind., a hair stylist gave him a free hair cut and called a reporter from the South Bend Tribune. After interviewing him and taking photographs, the reporter asked him if he would carry the film into South Bend to the newspaper.

Sweetgall has passed from the ecstasy of Michigan's Detroit Tigers fans to the mourning of Chicago Cubs fans, but no one has talked about Sunday's Reagan-Mondale debate. He said, "It's all baseball. I haven't heard one conversation about the debate."

His collection of money found along the side of the road, including deposit returns, has increased to $21.08.

*Oct. 11, 1984* ——————————— *Week 5*

BROOKLYN, Wisc. — Sunday night in Chicago, Ill, Robert Sweetgall's fortune cookie said, "You will soon make a trip over the desert."

Tuesday morning the cold and rain came. The rain started near Harvard, Ill., and worsened as he got crossed from Big Foot, Ill, into the state of Wisconsin. "Just as I got to the Welcome to Wisconsin sign, the thunder and lightning started. It poured for eight miles," he said, "with thin rivers flooding across the asphalt, the sides of the road muddy, the trucks spraying rooser tails of water onto my shoes."

Because his feet were wet, the callouses he had built up started to peel (a condition he does not relish because it makes his feet more susceptible to blisters). But he is feeling healthy and strong, he said.

The land in Wisconsin is mostly flat, with many farms and a lot of corn. "A lot of black earth, red barns and silos," Sweetgall said yesterday.

The weather has turned colder, with morning temperatures in the 30s, warming up to the low 40s. The sunrise yesterday had a hint of orange against light blue skies, he said, but later changed to clouds and showers.

Sweetgall said he planned to walk yesterday from about 15 miles southwest of Janesville, Wis., to about 15 miles on the other side of the city, near Fort Atkinson, where he would spend last night.

But Tuesday was the big day. "I did 41 miles, my biggest mileage day so far, crossing from Illinois to Wisconsin. I got a real early start and the weather was cold, which makes it easier to walk," he said.

It was only the second day of the journey on which he was able to make his "dream goal" of 20 miles before noon. 'If I can do that, it spells an easy afternoon and early evening," he said. "Unfortunately, I've only been getting in 12 or 14 miles before noon and not ending the day until close to 9 or 10 at night."

He also discovered Pino's Pizza, near Darien. "A full spaghetti dinner. It must have been two pounds, with mozzarella cheese melted on it and bread -- $1.75," Sweetgall said.

"The owner, Carmello, who has a Frankie Avalon haircut and was wearing a red t-shirt, said he came here about 10 years ago from Italy. He wouldn't take any money. Then he sent his son home to get a hairdryer so I could dry my shoes."

A motel owner outside Darien who said he "hadn't put anybody up in years," put Sweetgall up Tuesday night. He said, "He and his wife were very nice, but the waitress at the cafe in the morning was stunned when she found out he had put me up for nothing."

Last Friday Sweetgall underwent testing at the University of Massachusetts Medical Center here and at the university's exercise sciences and nutrition department in Amherst.

He has found $22.45 in change along the road. "Illinois was one of the poorest states as far as finding change," he said. "I found less than a dollar. In Barrington, one of the richest towns in Illinois, a real ritzy town, I found 3 cents."

*Oct. 18, 1984* ——————————— *Week 6*

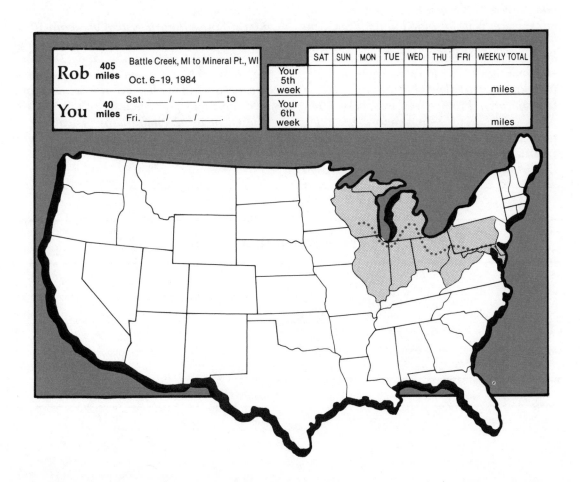

| | | SAT | SUN | MON | TUE | WED | THU | FRI | WEEKLY TOTAL |
|---|---|---|---|---|---|---|---|---|---|
| **Rob** 405 miles | Battle Creek, MI to Mineral Pt., WI  Oct. 6–19, 1984 | Your 5th week | | | | | | | miles |
| **You** 40 miles | Sat. ___/___/___ to  Fri. ___/___/___. | Your 6th week | | | | | | | miles |

### 5 Walking Research

My air shuttles back to Boston for research testing were tougher than the walk, mostly due to flight stress. After arriving at Logan Airport, I was shuttled 40 miles to U. Mass Medical Center (Worcester), fed macaroni, soggy carrots, and jello—and put to bed. Sleep was 4 hours—until 4 a.m.—at which time my head was encapsulated in a plastic breathing box for basal metabolism tests. At about 7 a.m. a catheter needle got shoved up my forearm vein for blood sampling. Ouch! Then I'd hop on a motorized treadmill for a 2-hour stress EKG test—my chest pasted with electrodes and a 6" long thermometer wire (vaseline dipped) planted in my rectum (core temperature). Probing research. The afternoon was full of X-rays, more breathing tests, leg muscle measurements and a 2-hour ride to Amherst (U. Mass. Exercise Science Department). There I was dunked 8 to 10 times in a tank of warm chlorinated water for body fat determination. Last came the high-speed filming of my low-speed walking. The midnight express took me back to Boston for 5 hours of sleep and my morning return flight to my last point of progress. Then I'd resume the walk. Thank God!

After 11,208 miles of walking and 8 of these research experiences, I found out that 3.5 mph easy-gaited walking: (1) improved my cardiorespiratory system by about 10%, (2) lowered my body fat composition and overall weight significantly, and (3) helped maintain my blood serum cholesterol at a relatively low, safe value. All this without one detectable injury—even after completing the equivalent of 428 marathons of walking in 364 straight days. What does that tell you about walking?

### 6 Your Personal Foot Notes

12

# Mississippi Bluffs

Photo by The Dassel Dispatch.

**Halloween Portrait**   It was great making friends along the way—friends like the Hollys whom I met on my 1982–83 trek. On this 1984 Halloween, we took a trick-or-treat mug shot in Litchfield, MN. Pictured left to right are Bob Holly, Buck (who walked 9 miles in freezing mist with me), Cody (Count Dracula), Jake (The Incredible Hulk on my shoulders), Josh (Dracula II), Carol (mother), and Sunshine (a sweet witch).

# Corn, Hogs and Strong Air

PRESTON, Minn. — Route 52 north.

Morning temperatures have been in the low- to mid-20s, and he has been hearing warnings of winter.

"You can't take those warnings lightly. I think I'm going to order some snow shoes and have them sent to a post office ahead in case I might need them," Robert J. Sweetgall said in a telephone interview yesterday. "You just can't predict the weather here. It can change so fast."

A two- or three-foot snowfall would slow him down, but Sweetgall said he is more concerned that he might pull a muscle while walking through deep snow. With his tight schedule of about 100 speaking engagements along the walk, an injury could mean disaster, causing a domino effect that could jeopardize the tour.

One of the towns through which he walked, Barneveld, Wisc, was struck by a tornado June 8 that killed nine persons. It also hit the nearby small community of Black Earlh. "The town is devasted. Words can't describe it. The tornado hit at midnight with no warning and 300 mile per hour winds," Sweetgall said. "One man said it sounded like a jet crashing outside."

Sweetgall walked through rain five of six days in Illinois and Wisconsin. He said the beehive hair dryer at the Hairport Beauty Salon in Verona, Wisc., last week did a fine job drying his shoes.

But the weather the past few days has been cold and often overcast. "I'm getting into weather I like, cool and crisp, with fiery red-orange sunsets and purple-red sunrises," Sweetgall said.

He has had no blisters in the last 1,100 miles, which he said is unusual. He has walked a total of 1,445 miles since leaving Newark, Del., on Sept. 7. "My feet are sore at night," he said, "but they recover."

He enjoys the night walking. "There's a lot of peace out here. And the Iowa air, it smells either clean and fresh or of pigs," he said and laughed. "The roads are good, concrete with wide shoulders. But the big stones cause problems with my ankles and force me to walk on the concrete.

"The view from Rickardsville, outside of Dubuque, Iowa, is the most spectacular sight yet. It overlooks the valley, looking down on 100 to 200 farms — blue Harvestore silos, red barns, white farm houses, green pastures. you can see for 40 miles.

"This is some of the hilliest country in the U.S., almost like West Virginia. It's also some of the most productive farm land in the world — dairy, grain, hogs. The electric clock outside the Luana (Iowa) Savings Bank gives time, temperature, the price of corn — $2.69 a bushel — and the price of hogs," Sweetgall said.

"Most of these are small towns, 50 to 200 people, with some of the larger ones having 3,000 to 4,000 people. Most consist of a gas station, feed store and tavern, some with grocery stores," he said.

Tuesday's 48.8 mile walk at 3.8 miles per hour (he started at 6 a.m. and stopped for the night at 11:15 p.m., including stops) was the longest in one day and put him one half day ahead of schedule.

In Luxemburg, he stopped at the same tavern shop he stopped at during his U.S. perimeter walk in 1982-83. "I had the same meal, in the same place, with the same conversation I had on a Thursday night in May 1983. Cheese on a hamburger bun done in a microwave oven," Sweetgall said.

"I said to the man, who remembered me, 'How much?'

"He said, 'Gimme a buck.' Same thing he said last time."

Sweetgall said his count of change found on the roads is $22.94 with only 14 cents found along the roads of the otherwise fertile Iowa.

*Oct. 25, 1984* ——————————— *Week 7*

LITCHFIELD, Minn. — Robert Sweetgall calls this the "acid test."

From here to Seattle, Wash. — the next 56 days — probably will be the roughest weather days he will find on the tour. "Due west through North Dakota, South Dakota, Montana, Idaho and central Washington.

The temperature this morning was 9 degrees, with an official wind chill factor of minus 15 degrees. "The wind is about 25 miles per hour out of the west, right in my face," Sweetgall said this morning. "I've got double layers of everything on.

"Yesterday was the first day of snow, but they were just flurries," he said.

He has walked through rain 13 days on the tour, most of it in the past two weeks. But he said the rain is at an end. "It doesn't usually rain here this time of the year," Sweetgall said, "it snows."

In Dassell Tuesday he picked up a package containing his winter weather gear: a balaclava face mask; a pure wool hat; a longsleeve turtleneck shirt; wool longsleeve shirt (the three shirts will be worn for layering effect) and wool walking pants.

Also, a Gore-Tex walking suit; a pair of wool mittens; gloves and Gore-Tex mittens; a wool dickie; six pairs of double layer socks and two pair of waterproof socks.

"For the next 56 days, 1,700 miles, I'll be walking into sunsets at night if I'm lucky, freezing rain or snow if I'm not," he said. "I expect the mornings and nights to be sub-freezing temperatures with wind chills well below freezing. And I don't expect to see any days over 40 degrees."

Monday in Minneapolis ("Very clean, not like your average big city.") Sweetgall spoke at two elementary schools, had two live television in-terviews, one television filming, three radio interviews, two newspaper interviews and spoke to the Rotary Club.

Tuesday night he went to a haunted house run by a civic organization in Howard Lake. "It's the only entertainment I've allowed myself on this tour," he said. A partition fell, landing less than 2 feet from his left foot.

The recent rains have flooded the corn and bean fields and left farmers unable to harvest their crops. "They need a freeze so they can get the tractors onto the fields," Sweetgall said.

"Ahead are Indian towns, cafe towns, a lot of farm land. It's kind of thin, with fewer motels so I will have to depend on people to put me up about half the time. In the next three weeks I won't see a city bigger than 25,000. And I'll cross the Sioux Indian Reservation within a week and a half, 60 miles across."

His loose change collection is $25.54.

*Nov. 1, 1984* ——————————————— *Week 8*

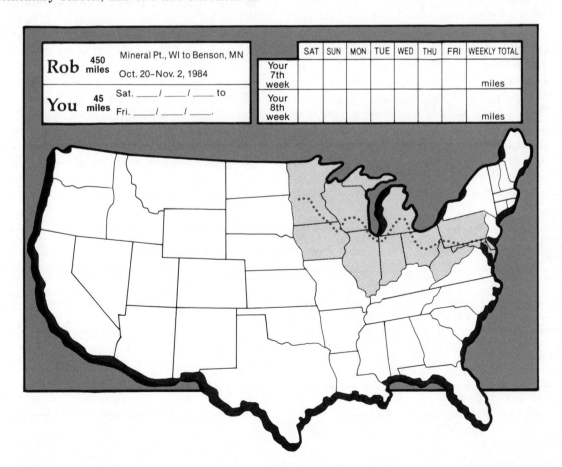

| | | SAT | SUN | MON | TUE | WED | THU | FRI | WEEKLY TOTAL |
|---|---|---|---|---|---|---|---|---|---|
| **Rob** 450 miles | Mineral Pt., WI to Benson, MN / Oct. 20–Nov. 2, 1984 | Your 7th week | | | | | | | | miles |
| **You** 45 miles | Sat. ___/___/___ to / Fri. ___/___/___. | Your 8th week | | | | | | | | miles |

7 **Thanking a Stranger**

How does a journeyman thank a stranger on the road for a great favor? That's what I asked "The King of the Hoboes" in Toledo. Steam Train replied: "Oh I'd just say something like, 'Well I'll just put a hobo blessing on your house, and the Good Lord, I hope he puts one on you too?'" He continued, "I speak to women senior citizen groups every weekend. And I'll say to them, 'How many of you have ever fed a hobo at your back door?' Most of them raise their hand. And I'll say, 'Do you remember feeding them? Yes, we always fed them. We'd never turn them away.' They'd want to tell me the stories. They even knew some of their names. And it was a happy thought in their hearts for many, many years. 'Yeah, I remember old crooked-nose Pete who used to come by our house. He was one of our best friends.' You see, old Pete left a blessing. When they fed him, they got a blessing out of it that stayed with them all their life."

Steam Train's philosophy made sense to me—especially in those awkward moments when I'd be standing in the doorway, ready to say good-by, wondering what to say to the couple who took me into their home the night before.

Late one afternoon near Kearney, NE, I knocked on the door of a roadside house. I was thirsty. When no one answered, I tried the door. It opened. Inside, a little hound dog sprung off the couch waking up Nick Ponticello, a 71 year old fitness guru who hardly knew his age. When I explained my story, he handed me his special guest book filled with the signatures and addresses of transcontinentalists and the dates of their crossings. Two hours of conversation later, Nick wished me a good night's sleep in his guest apartment.

When I thanked him, he responded: "Don't thank me. I met you, and you met me."

8 **Your Personal Foot Notes**

# Weeks 9 & 10

# Dakota

Photo by Ozzie Drager.

---

**Wind-whipped Walkers**
Along North Dakota's wheat and sunflower fields, were telephone poles, a grain elevator, and two cattle ranchers who thought it would be more fun to walk 101 miles across their state than to keep building a sheep barn. Danny Swartzwalter, Rob Sweetgall, and Dennis Johnson—46 miles completed, 55 miles yet to go. Just west of Reeder, population 306. November 15, 1984.

# Early Winter and The Long Walk West

ABERDEEN, S.D. — "Every single person is asking 'How are you going to cross North Dakota and Montana at this time of year?" Robert J. Sweetgall said. " I tell them I'm prepared and I'll just keep walking."

Had the walk been planned south instead of west to start, he would have had to walk across the central plains — Kansas, Mississippi and Nebraska — in January and February. He said, "It would have been worse weatherwise than going through North Dakota and Montana in November and December."

Sweetgall said he has been averaging 30 miles a day. Weather the past week has been good, with temperatures in the 30s with a lot of wind. Yesterday was 58. "A beautiful day, but too hot for me. Right now the ideal walking temperature is 25 to 30," he said.

"I've been eating a lot of canned mixed vegetables that I heat in microwaves in convenience stores," he said. "Much of the time I eat while I walk." The other night my supper was three cans of string beans. One lunch was four large hamburger rolls because that's all the store had. I'm looking forward to a salad bar in Aberdeen."

Breakfasts when possible, have consisted of pancakes or eggs (no yokes), with toast and a triple order of potatoes, one of his favorites. Sweetgall said he carried snacks such as bananas or a couple slices of bread for the walk.

He said that if he were uncertain whether he would find food ahead, he would buy a loaf of whole wheat bread and peanut butter and make himself four triple-decker sandwiches to carry. "Peanut butter is a good food because it offers a lot of calories, which I need," he said.

Sleeping arrangements have been uncertain. Friday night he slept in a grain elevator in Benson, Minn., a 25-pound bag of dog food for a pillow. Saturday night, 13 miles outside of Ortonville, Minn., a family let him sleep in the unfinished attic of their little grocery store-gas station, their children's winter coats offered as pillows.

"Now I start getting into real thin country — towns 20 to 30 miles apart, no motels. Dry prairie, rolling hills. Most of South Dakota was flat, tough, wheat and corn fields. They get about 15 inches of rain a year, but this year they got 24 inches," he said. "Saturday I start across the Sioux Indian Reservation."

In Andover, S.D., Tuesday, he walked into a "cafe-grocery store-pool hall building. There were six ladies sitting at a long table. The voting booths were made of plywood, sort of like phone booths. They were across from the jukebox and surrounded by groceries. The pool table was there, but the cafe was in the next room," he said.

"Andover, North and South, has 185 registered voters and the women said 166 had voted by 7:30 p.m. They said the election was real close and they were all excited to count the votes.

"In the cafe five old farmers sat watching television and they said why should anyone bother voting now," Sweetgall said. "They were very cynical. They said the networks shouldn't broadcast the votes until the next day. And in the next room the women couldn't wait to get started counting."

Reagan won Andover with 110 votes to Mondale's 65.

Sweetgall's loose change collection is at $26.70.

*Nov. 8, 1984* ———————————— *Week 9*

HETTINGER, N.D. — It's a race, of sorts.

Robert J. Sweetgall first met Earl and Lorraine Roebuck 18 months ago on his 10,000 walk-run of the country's perimeter. He stayed with them last Saturday at their home in Java, S.D.

He may see them again Jan. 23 when he passes the house to which they are moving on Route 99 in Gault, Calif., about 40 miles south of Sacramento. "I told them it's a race. I plan to walk there before they can sell their house and move there.

"They now live on top of a hill right on the 100th meridian. It's really out in the country," Sweetgall said in a telephone call yesterday. "I stopped there Friday night. Their two dogs came running down to the chicken wire fence barking and jumping, so I didn't dare climb over to go up to the house.

"It was dark and there were a few clouds and a little yellow circle of a full moon. It didn't give much light. I called Earl's name but the wind would blow it back in my face. Finally he came down to the fence and got me. He said he recognized my voice the first time he heard me call."

Sweetgall may be the swiftest in the Java-to-Gault race since the Roebucks must sell their 7-bedroom home, two barns and 12 acres ($28,000), then move themselves and son Kelly, three cars, two dozen deer, 25 wild geese, a flock of pigeons, 12 pheasants, two cats and two dogs. He said Roebuck plans to move the animals in his van.

There have been few people and many open miles in the past week's walk through South Dakota. Last Thursday morning Sweetgall stopped in Mina, S.D., population 23. The town celebrated its 100 birthday a year ago and 5,000 people came to celebrate. It consists of a grocery (another microwave vegetable breakfast), welding shop and post office.

The big towns, like Morristown, population 50, have a bank," Sweetgall said.

As he crossed the Missouri River in Mobridge he crossed into Mountain time and shorter days and the Sioux Indian reservation. "I visited with an old Indian named W.A. Sherwood. His mailbox is an old 1895 toilet taken from Fort Yates.

He told me that where I'm heading into, Montana, even the jack rabbits carry box lunches.

The Indian territory was "desolate," really, mostly sagebrush and prairie grass. It's a world of three colors: blue sky, beige prairie and black asphalt."

The wind has been so strong in some places he said he has had to walk in the ditch which is about four feet below the road surface and runs along the road.

Sweetgall's lunches have been his mainstay of peanut butter and jelly sandwiches carried in a plastic bag tied to his waist. Peanut butter has seemed like a luxury compared to some of the fare.

Yesterday, today and tomorrow he is being accompanied by ranchers Dennis Johnson and Danny Schwarzwalter. Sweetgall is staying with Johnson and his wife Linda in Reeder (pop. 306).

His loose change collection stands at $27.61

*Nov. 15, 1984* ——————————— *Week 10*

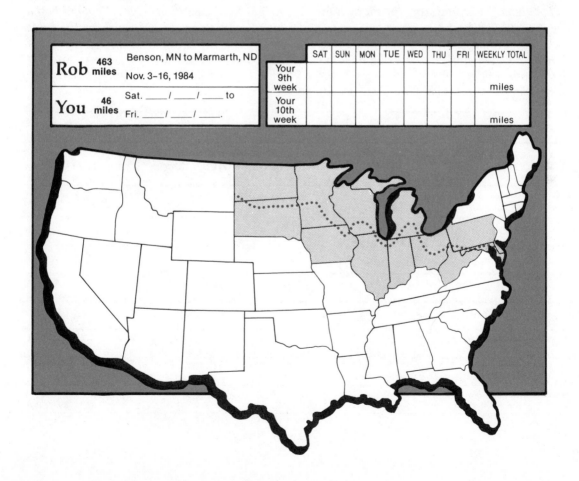

| Rob 463 miles | Benson, MN to Marmarth, ND | | SAT | SUN | MON | TUE | WED | THU | FRI | WEEKLY TOTAL |
|---|---|---|---|---|---|---|---|---|---|---|
| | Nov. 3–16, 1984 | Your 9th week | | | | | | | | miles |
| You 46 miles | Sat. ___/___/___ to | Your 10th week | | | | | | | | |
| | Fri. ___/___/___. | | | | | | | | | miles |

# Foot Notes

## 9   In Search of Loose Change

*The only time I ever found money on the highway was when I looked for it. Sounds ridiculous? Maybe it is. But a lot of walkers don't look. That's why our streets are loaded with copper and silver pieces—enough so that I totaled a tax-exempt profit of $182.82 for 50 states. I call it "picker-uppers". You pick up a coin, and it picks up your mood. It kind of brings out the kid in you: "Gee! Look what I found!" Keeping score on a long journey—or on a lifetime walking program—adds a new dimension. It gives you something to do, something to think about, something more than "miles," "minutes," and "heart rates". You can see your slow, steady progress—penny by penny, dollar by dollar.*

*The best part is that it's so unpredictable. In some of the richest areas of the country such as Palm Springs, California (my first trek), I found next to nothing. What does that tell you? Yet along Montana's eastern prairie, the Old Yellowstone Highway, I came up with several dollars in coins! Kansas was great for quarters. The Mojave Desert was rich in Roosevelt dimes. New England had a lot of everything, as did much of the Bible Belt. But it really doesn't matter; I just think it's kind of nice when you can turn a long 35-mile day of walking into finding 16 cents.*

## 10   Your Personal Foot Notes

# Big Sky

Photo by Patsy Almy.

**On the Prairie** In Ismay, Montana, population 21, children still go to country schools. At the Whitney Creek Schoolhouse, the cows (who share the schoolyard pasture) move off to a nearby grazing area when the kids walk outside at recess. Pictured are: 1st grade—Richard, Scotti, and Jeremy; 2nd grade— Melissa; 3rd grade—Tim and Matt; 4th grade—Tom; 5th grade—Robert; 6th grade— Tanya; 7th grade—Melvin; and teacher Ms. Jolene Langin and her 3-year-old Alaskan Malamute dog.

# Cold Mornings on Montana's Prairie

POMPEYS PILLAR, Mont. — "Perfect 60 degree weather: 10 degrees in the morning, 30 degrees during the day and 20 degrees at night," Robert Sweetgall said.

Sweetgall is walking alone again, after spending three days last week walking with Dennis Johnson and Danny Schwarzwalter, two Reeder (pop. 350), North Dakota ranchers who walked 101 miles across their state and into Montana with him last week.

Sweetgall was put up by Johnson and his wife Linda, a school teacher, on his walk-run of the United States perimeter two years ago. This year, Mrs. Johnson arranged Sweetgall's North Dakota speaking engagements for him.

In a telephone interview, Johnson said he and Schwarzwalter are joggers, running about 15 to 25 miles a week. "We are fitness minded and we thought it would be quite a challenge to walk with Rob. Also, Rob spends a lot of time alone on the road and we thought he might enjoy it. It would let us spend some time with him.

"We thought the walk wouldn't be that tough, but it's going to take us a week and a half to get back into shape. I've never been under such physical stress," said Johnson, 43. "We were really hurting physically — our ankles were swollen, we've got blisters, tendonitis, leg muscles knotted up.

Johnson said the first day the three walked together, Nov. 15, the wind was blowing strongly with gusts up to 60 miles an hour. "I think that might have taken its toll. It was very difficult walking in it. Over the three days, we made the 101 miles in about 30 hours of walking, or about 3.3 miles per hour," he said.

Sweetgall said eastern Montana consisted of "cattle prairie, a lot of barbed wire, rusty brown lava rock. There's a lot of deer and coyote, which I hear at night but haven't seen."

The schools are often small. The Cottonwood School has 12 pupils, the Knowlton School has six and the Fertile Prairie School in Baker, where he spoke on his first trip, has six. "One room, one teacher."

Sweetgall said the people here and in North Dakota "are laid back, very friendly. As someone said, out here the people just leave the keys in the car and make sure there's enough gas in case you need to use it. One housewife called every rancher along the route for miles ahead to let them know I was coming. I felt guilty if I didn't stop by to let them know I was fine," he said.

"One of the most spectacular things I have ever seen was the Northern Lights, which I saw last Thursday (Nov. 15). They were like icicles hanging out of the sky, a white dripping curtain just hanging there. It was beautiful."

Sweetgall said the roads are rough and cracked but paved with silver. "So far, Montana leads the nation in loose change. I've already found $1.89 here for a total of $30.24.

*Nov. 23, 1984* ——————————— *Week 11*

COLUMBUS, Mont. — Robert Sweetgall is one-third of the way across Montana, 260 miles into a state that he liked and believes is misunderstood. It is not, he insists, as barren or windswept as people may believe.

"The big sky, that's what they call it and what's what you see out here. It's very friendly," he said, "and the weather isn't as bad. Also, it gets more gorgeous as you get further into it."

It also gets higher. "The next nine days are all uphill, against the wind. This middle section of the state along the yellowstone River is the toughest part because of the wind," Sweetgall said.

"This is the start of the Continental Divide, which I plan to cross next Wednesday.

Sweetgall said he will cross the divide at McDonald's Pass (elevation 6,325 feet), just west of Helena, the state capital. "The climb starts at about a one or two percent grade and goes to a six to eight percent grade," he said. It's about 18 miles up the east side of the pass and eight miles down to the nearest town on the west, he said.

"At the top it just blows crazy. Swirling winds. There's always snow blowing whether it's snowing or not. But it's a tremendous sight. You can see 100 mountain ranges if it's a half clear day. In the first town on the other side is a place called the Last Chance Tavern. Sounds like a good place to celebrate the climb," Sweetgall said.

At noon on Thanksgiving, he "watched a little brown dog chase a big black dog down the main street in Custer. It was deserted. Everything was closed. I ate a strawberry jam on whole wheat sandwich and drank a Dr. Pepper from a machine as I was sitting on the concrete stoop at an Exxon station."

Later, he was taken to a Thanksgiving dinner by a family which had put him up the previous night. He said he ate "pumpkin pie, stuffing, cottage cheese and lots of vegetables."

On Monday, Sweetgall underwent the second testing period at the University of Massachusetts Medical Center and the university's exercise and nutrition science department in Amherst. He returns to Worcester about every seven weeks for testing to determine the effects of walking on the body.

Sweetgall said he knows a few people in Montana from his 1982-83 perimeter tour of the country, but he said has not made any advance sleeping arrangements. "As long as I can see lights of towns while I'm out on a highway at night, I'm not too worried."

He said he was worried briefly about snakes, but he got over that. "A guy in a tavern warned me to look out for snow snakes, which are poisonous. He said they'll kill you faster than a train," Sweetgall said. "They're white and wiggle through the snow, leaving small tracks. I told some friends about it, but when they started laughing I knew I had been taken."

His loose change collection suffered from the trip back east, and now stands at $30.91, he said.

*Nov. 29, 1984* —————————————— *Week 12*

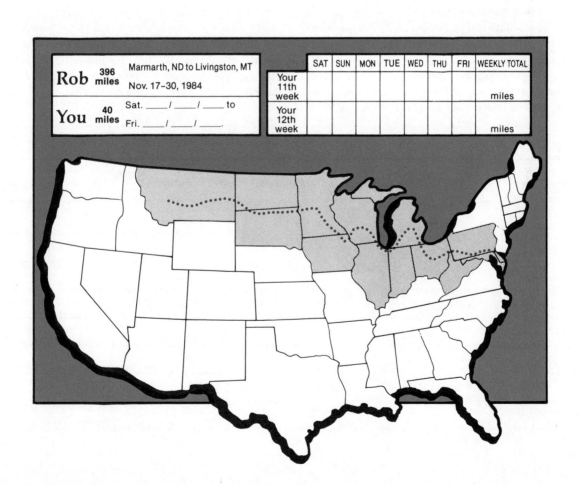

| | | SAT | SUN | MON | TUE | WED | THU | FRI | WEEKLY TOTAL |
|---|---|---|---|---|---|---|---|---|---|
| **Rob** 396 miles | Marmarth, ND to Livingston, MT — Nov. 17–30, 1984 | | | | | | | | |
| **You** 40 miles | Sat. ___/___/___ to — Fri. ___/___/___. | | | | | | | | |
| Your 11th week | | | | | | | | | miles |
| Your 12th week | | | | | | | | | miles |

# Foot Notes Weeks 11 & 12

## 11 Keeping a Walking Journal

My fanny pack was so small that I really did some soul-searching in selecting items for my journey. Traveling light. Things such as my 35 mm school slide show, travelers' checks ($1500), my footcare kit, road maps, and storm gear were critical, I figured. Changes of clothing were not. So I simply learned to strip real fast in laundramats while patrons had their backs turned. My wool underlayers went into the washer; my Gore-Tex shell became my new public bathrobe. Forty minutes later, I'd reverse the wash-dress cycle. I never got arrested either.

Instead of spare clothing, I carried extra sheets of papers, a microcassette tape recorder, and a few dozen magnetic tapes. These items were my walking diary. Keeping such a journal was an investment in the future—something to fall back on in my old age. I made daily records of my road travels—the people, the land, the feelings and conversations. My paper logs, I mailed back East. The microcassette tapes I personally deposited in a bank vault on my return trips to Worcester. It was always tough at the moment to make time for a journal entry. But it was worth it.

As your eyes move down this page, you'll see a blank space below. You can leave it blank, or you can fill it in. It's your choice. It just depends on how much of your life you'll care to recall 10 or 20 years from now.

## 12 Your Personal Foot Notes

_____

_____

_____

_____

_____

_____

_____

# The Continental Divide

**Rocky Mountain High**
Climbing the Continental Divide sent a chill down my back. At the top, you can see the world—where you've been and where you're going. For a journeyman, it's "progress" and "beauty" wrapped into one. For these Helena, Montana students who climbed McDonald Pass (elev. 6325'), it's much the same. December 5, 1984.

Photo by Frank Shone.

# Climbing Uphill on Ice to Lookout Pass

ELLISTON, Mont. — "It was a good day for the Divide," Robert Sweetgall said. "Clear and windy, about 17 degrees. All you could see were evergreen-lined mountain ranges with snowcaps on top. It was beautiful."

Sweetgall yesterday walked across the Continental Divide, the ridge of the Rocky Mountains that separates rivers flowing in an easterly direction from those flowing in a westerly direction, at McDonald's Pass (elevation 6,325 feet).

He made the crossing with Bruce Katz, president of Rockport Shoe Co. of Marlboro, one of the sponsors of the year-long walk. Sweetgall said he had challenged Katz to make the crossing with him last summer while finalizing plans for the walk."

Sweetgall and Katz were joined by about 80 students from two Helena schools who were bused up the pass to walk the last two miles with the walkers.

"The morning temperatures have been about zero or slightly below, which is a little uncomfortable, especially for my fingers and nose. But it warms up during the day and is very nice," he said.

However, it was so cold when he crossed the Bozeman Pass Saturday that he said he couldn't take off his gloves to retie his shoes.

"I got 18 unsolicited offers for rides that day," Sweetgall said. "On normal days I might get anywhere from zero to nine ride offers. If I get 10 to 20 offers, it's a nasty day. If I get over 20 offers of rides, it usually means the going is so bad I shouldn't be out there."

On Thursday he passed through Grey Cliff, where an old sheep herder found a treasure buried by Jesse James after a train robbery. "The town's just some weatherbeaten old buildings and a few decent houses now," he said.

On Friday, he spoke at a school in Big Timber. "None of the 34 staff members smoke. Those teachers are great role models for the kids."

On the highway outside of Big Timber he saw a sign that said school zone, hopped a fence (and ripped his Gore-Tex running suit) and walked up to a white building with a green roof and an old school bell on top. The Springdale School had eight students ("They're losing a sixth grader this year, but two kindergarten pupils are coming in.)"

He spoke to the students about 25 minutes then played a game of kickball with them on the frozen Montana turf. "I've played punch ball, stick ball and stoop ball," said Sweetgall, a Brooklyn, N.Y., native. "But I've never played kickball. Dusty Plum, a sixth grader, got a triple off of me." Sweetgall then jumped the fence back to the highway and continued walking.

There has been only about an inch of snow in the past week, although there's snow on the ground everywhere. The walking has been kind of slippery," he said.

On his walk-jog around the U.S. perimeter in 1982 and 1983 he fell eight times, three of them in Livingston. Friday night he fell for the first time on this walk — in Livingston.

Sunday afternoon he ate lunch at the Prairie Schooner Cafe in Three Forks with owner Joyce Brown's dog Slick, a Doberman pinscher, sitting with him throughout the meal — "real nice dog."

There is little change on the icy roads, Sweetgall said, and his loose change collection is at $31.10.

*Dec. 6, 1984* —————————————— *Week 13*

COEUR D'ALENE, Idaho — "As you're walking down the road you look up at the mountains, straight up. You think they're going to fall on top of you," Robert Sweetgall said.

"They're tall, tall mountains with a spiking carpet of evergreens, topped with fresh, powdered snow. I can't think of anything in Vermont that matches this."

Sweetgall has finished his 24-day walk through Montana, crossing Look Out Pass Tuesday from Saltese, Mont. to Mullan, Idaho and into the Pacific Time Zone. In the past week he has walked 275 miles along Interstate 90 through Helena, Goldcreek, Bearmouth, Missoula, Frenchtown, Phosphate and De Borgia, Mont. He has walked 2,992 miles since he left Delaware in September.

Tonight he should cross into Washington state, heading to Greenacres. He has the three school assemblies plus news interviews scheduled for tomorrow in Spokane, Wash.

The weather has warmed during the past week, from zero and below to the 20s and 30s. It's too warm for Sweetgall, who said those temperatures cause his feet to become hot and red.

Since leaving Missoula on Saturday, it has been fog, mist, freezing rain and snow. "The roads have been solid ice," he said. "The shoulders of the roads are iced with crunchy crater ice, bending the ankles when you walk on it. I've been walking in the left lane, real close to traffic. The trucks have been traveling about 10 miles per hour so they won't overturn.

Much of the past week has been spent in small towns. Friday he stayed in Phosphate, Mont. (pop. 20), with Roy Burke, a retired Burlington and Northern Railroad worker and his wife Mae. The spike that joined the railroads east and west lines had been driven outside the window in the bedroom where he slept.

Saturday he stayed at Rock Creek Lodge, outside of Missoula, Mont., owned by Rodney Abraham Lincoln, a fourth generation descendant of Abraham Lincoln.

On Saturday, his 37th birthday, Sweetgall walked through Missoula, "the most polluted city so far on the tour." He said the pollution is caused by a nearby paper pulp factory and the smoke from wood stoves.

"It's beautiful there, but it's in a valley and the air is stagnant. You almost gag walking down the highway," he said. "It's a perfect example of man ruining the environment."

Sweetgall said the first malicious incident he has encountered was on Sunday when a truck drove into the breakdown lane to spray him with ice and water as he rested against a guardrail. A chunk of ice hit his shin, but he was not injured.

Sunday he competed 50.5 miles, the biggest day on the tour, in a cold, drizzling rain. He had gone through all eight pairs of socks that day, and the hotel owner dried them in a dryer for him.

Sweetgall said that despite the icy and snow covered roads, his loose change collection has risen 80 cents to $31.90.

*Dec. 13, 1984* ——————————— *Week 14*

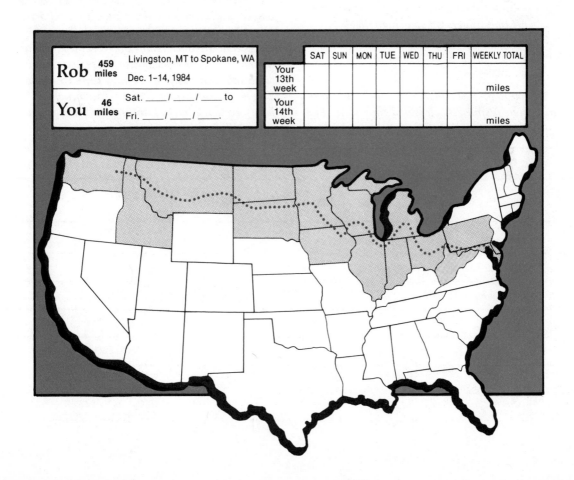

| | | SAT | SUN | MON | TUE | WED | THU | FRI | WEEKLY TOTAL |
|---|---|---|---|---|---|---|---|---|---|
| **Rob** 459 miles | Livingston, MT to Spokane, WA<br>Dec. 1–14, 1984 | | | | | | | | |
| **You** 46 miles | Sat. ___/___/___ to<br>Fri. ___/___/___. | Your 13th week | | | | | | | miles |
| | | Your 14th week | | | | | | | miles |

**13**  The Friendly Factor _____

Facing traffic on my walks, I often waved "hello" to motorists. Sometimes they waved back. Sometimes they drove by stone-faced. Other times I received worse responses. The whole thing got me curious as to which regions of the country were the most friendly. So I developed a "point scoring system" on the highway that went as follows:

- **1 point**—*full-out wave or big smile*
- **½ point**—*token acknowledgment (motorists lift two fingers off steering wheel).*
- **0 points**—*no response*
- **– 1 point**—*negative expression*
- **– 2 points**—*malicious or obscene gesture*

I'd wave to 100 consecutive motorists and tally their responses. (It killed time too!) The total number of points for those 100 vehicles I named "THE FRIENDLY FACTOR".

Near Helena, Montana, I was pulling Friendly Factors (FF) of "45" to "55". Northern California backroads had high FF's in the mid 60's. But coming into Missoula, Montana, on I–90, the traffic scored a poor "21". Why the "21"? The more I tried to correlate my "FF" scores with "Regional Friendliest"—well, it just wasn't working. Then something struck me. The highest "FF" scores came on roads where traffic moved the slowest. Similarly, low FF's occurred on high-speed thoroughfares like I–90 outside of Missoula. That made sense. The slower motorists were not in so much of a rush—they had time to wave. The rat race crowd was in too much of a hurry to wave back. Funny—isn't it that way in real life?

**14**  Your Personal Foot Notes

_____

_____

_____

_____

_____

_____

_____

# The Evergreen State

Photo by Nadra Rivers.

**Crossing the Cascades**
Leaving the Bavarian-styled village of Leavenworth, WA, Highway 2 took me on a winding uphill tour of Tumwater Canyon for 35 miles through snowy winter wonderlands to the top of Stevens Pass. Then it was all downhill in slush and gray misting skies to Seattle.

# Washington's Winter Wheatland—Burrrrr

WENATCHEE, Wash. — The wires sing, but it's a bitter song as winter takes bites out of Robert Sweetgall.

"There's irrigated farming here so they have pipelines that run across the fields and the winds are vibrating the pipes like crazy, almost like they are shivering. And you can hear the wind howling on the telephone lines.

"The wind is ferocious," he said in a telephone call yesterday. "On Tuesday the wind chill was 30 degrees below with the wind coming out of the west right at me. It felt like the wind was taking chunks out of my face. I had everything on but the wind got around it.

"It took me two-and-a-half hours to recuperate from a mile and a half walk from Coulee City and Dry Falls Tuesday morning before I got to Route 17 and headed south."

The roads are icy, but sometimes the biggest problem is seeing where he is going. "In a storm the sky is a whitish-grey and the fields are ivory white. Everything blends together. It's like walking in an eggshell. It was making me dizzy," he said.

The wind came with a Sunday night snowstorm that closed roads and gave Sweetgall his hardest, coldest walk of the trip, forcing him to alter his route. On Monday, he walked to Almira, population 349 (638 entered in last year's Great Almira Run) to find schools closed. "I got into town frozen. The highway was drifted with snow," he said. "It looked like a white conveyor belt sweeping across the highway."

Although there was no major accumulation, snow scrapers continually drove up and down the highway. "I found out later they have to do that because in less than an hour they can end up with a two foot drift where there had been no snow," Sweetgall said.

Leaving Almira, he hit an icy patch -- "the wind was about 20 miles an hour out of the north as I was going south." The wind caused him two hard falls that left his hip and elbow sore and black and blue. "It was high winds to Hartline," he said.

Sweetgall is protecting his face and feet with pure lanolin. On his head he wears a Gore-Tex balaklava with a neck extender that reaches under his three wool shirts; a 100 percent wool hat and hood and a wool dickie. But still the skin beneath his eyes is freezing.

Tuesday morning he faced 35-mile-per-hour winds coming directly off Route 2 in Coulee City. "The wind was forming white caps on Bank Lake, with frozen slush and ice floating like a waterbed blanket," he said.

"At 5 a.m. I looked out the window at the newspaper office and saw the Christmas lights bobbing up and down."

Sweetgall decided to change his route to walk south along Route 17 to Soap Lake then west and north on Route 28 rather than into the bleak empty miles of Route 2 to Waterville.

"I asked a man if there was any food between Coulee City and Soap Lake and he said, 'Not unless you fish.'" So at a small convenience store he had the owner spread six ounces of peanut butter on a loaf of bread before he began his walk south.

Sweetgall said he has not considered taking a day off. "I'm in good shape."

His loose change collection is $33.17.

*Dec. 20, 1984 —————————————— Week 15*

TACOMA, Wash. — Christmas Day for Robert J. Sweetgall was a 40-mile walk from Seattle to Tacoma "along an industrial highway where the only places to eat were 24-hour plastic menu restaurants.

With precipitation at a minimum, Christmas was one of the easiest days Sweetgall had this past week. It was a week during which the temperature hovered around zero on the eastern slope of the Cascade range and he was alternately forced to walk in snow and freezing rain.

But yesterday, sitting in a motel room in Tacoma hanging his feet out the door "to air," Sweetgall took some pleasure in recounting his most recent adventures. He has traveled 3,402 to date, with the latest stretch taking him through miles of snow-covered Washington State orchards, across the rugged Cascades and into Seattle on Christmas Eve.

He made it to the base of the Cascades by Thursday night where he stayed in Cashmere, Wash. — a small tourist town of about 1,000 people. There he had an encounter with a highway patrolman who rather curtly demanded he not walk in the street, even though Sweetgall said the sidewalks were either unshoveled or icy.

Heading into the mountains Friday, Sweetgall was greeted by Greg Peck and his elementary school students from the town of Leavenworth, Wash. Most of the school came out and walked with him about a mile and listened to an impromptu talk Sweetgall gave in a parking lot.

Knowing Sweetgall wouldn't make the 35 miles to Stevens' Pass that day, Peck had given Sweetgall the name of a friend who lived on the mountain. Sweetgall made it to the small house that night and slept on the floor, with his feet under a Christmas tree, alongside an English sheepdog named Argon.

The climb up to Stevens' Pass on Saturday morning through driving snow and slush wasn't an easy one for Sweetgall. He walked 15 miles to the top of the pass in ankle-deep slush which soaked his shoes through.

Saturday night found him at the Cascadia Hotel in Skykomish, Wash., where he said he was too beat to mind that the bed was shaped like a banana. By Sunday the rain had stopped and Sweetgall was able to dry out his shoes in the oven of a bakery he found along the way.

By Monday morning he was on the outskirts of Seattle. Approaching the north side of the city he found a wallet containing $22 and identification for a someone named Cheryl Lynn. Although the wallet was bulky, Sweetgall carried it as he walked across Seattle and met with members of the Seattle news media.

That night, Christmas Eve, Sweetgall made contact with Cheryl Lynn's family. A grateful relative came to retrieve the wallet at the small motel where Sweetgall was staying, gave Sweetgall a $10 reward and informed him that the wallet would be wrapped and placed under the tree for the girl.

Sweetgall's loose change collection has reached $36.37.

AMY ZUCKERMAN

*Dec. 27, 1984 ——————————— Week 16*

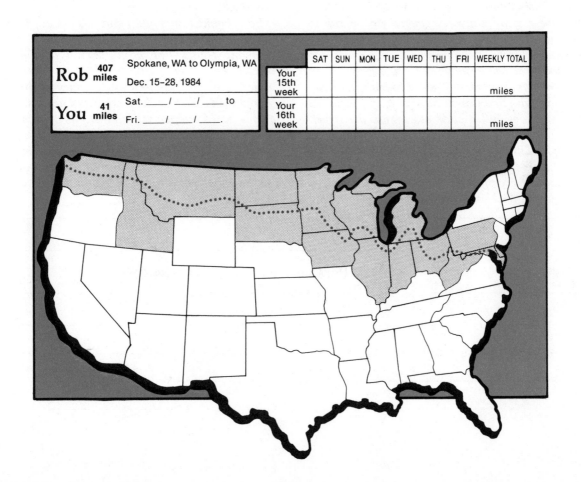

| | | Rob | 407 miles | Spokane, WA to Olympia, WA Dec. 15–28, 1984 | You | 41 miles | Sat. ____/____/____ to Fri. ____/____/____. |
|---|---|---|---|---|---|---|---|

| | SAT | SUN | MON | TUE | WED | THU | FRI | WEEKLY TOTAL |
|---|---|---|---|---|---|---|---|---|
| Your 15th week | | | | | | | | miles |
| Your 16th week | | | | | | | | miles |

# Foot Notes

# Weeks 15 & 16

**Ups and Downs** _____

On Day 6 of my trek, after six blisters, I slit open my shoes with a razor blade—"air conditioning." By Week 2, I was regularly slipping off my shoes and socks in restaurants—discretely of course. Waitresses rarely raised a stink, as long as I didn't. The trick is to ask permission politely. Also, tip accordingly. Acting so, I was only thrown out of three eating establishments on tour.

One of those was in Reardon, Washington, where two waitresses ganged up on me to squeal to their owner as I sat harmlessly in a quiet corner of an empty dining room—so empty I never thought to ask permission. Mistake. Upon being asked to leave halfway through my warm cottage cheese, I laced up my shoes and headed out across the street. There I walked right into a 4H sidewalk bake sale. Thirty-five cents bought me 5 chocolate chip cookies, a wooden bridge chair, and a cool breeze off the snowy wheat fields across the road. Next thing I knew, a friendly mother was explaining to me all about how snow protects Russian winter wheat, and her small son was proudly revealing his secret recipe for "getting the most chocolate chips into a blob of dough." And my feet were loving every minute of that cool wheatland air. Finally it was time to redress the feet and keep the journey moving West. When you meet such nice people, it's hard to say good-by. But you must.

So I thanked the family and headed out to face the setting sun. It was the hour of the changing colors—the hour when I always thought best. That night my mind was entertained with fortunes and misfortunes of life on the road—how such positive and negative events could happen within instants of each other. It teaches you one thing: the negative states of depression, anxiety, sadness, disgust, rejection and worry are not the end of the world. They are just a few dark clouds quickly passing.

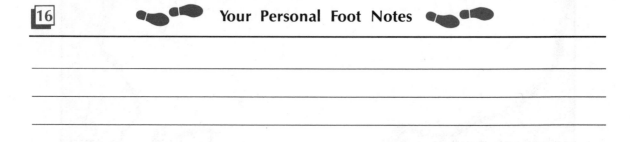

**Your Personal Foot Notes**

# Clean, Green Oregon

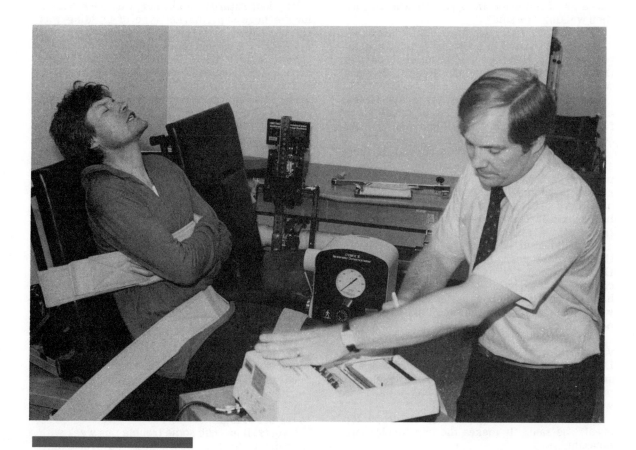

**No Respect** Back at U. of Mass. Physical Therapy Lab, I could never get any respect. Dr. Jim Michaels, the best humorist on the research team, would first critique my muscle flexibility. Next, he'd burn my legs out on his fancy Cybex muscle-testing apparatus. "At least you're not getting any worse" was one of his favorite lines.

# The Walk Enters Its' Second Year—1985

ST. HELENS, ORE. — Robert J. Sweetgall has time to relax now.

He's walking again.

Beginning with last Thursday's flight back to Worcester for medical testing, the past week has been one of sitting, waiting and flying, as he went from Seattle to Chicago to Boston to Worcester to Amherst to Boston to Anchorage to Seattle.

"I went through eight time zone changes, different altitudes, temperatures, humidity. There was a lot of confusion and stress. It was tougher than walking," he said.

"But the road's starting to straighten me out."

Sweetgall crossed into Oregon from Washington yesterday. He will spend about eight days in the state, reaching Portland tonight. He has walked about 150 miles in the past week.

The road here is through a landscape of low hills, tall evergreens and a lot of small horse farms. "Everything's green. Moss and mildew seem to grow around everything," he said.

The roads are sloped with ditches along their sides for water runoff, since it rains so often. A pleasant surprise, though, has been that it hasn't rained, Sweetgall said. The daily temperatures have been between 25 and 35, and the sky has been overcast. The forecasts have called for continued good weather.

A good deal of the planning for this trip over the past three years had involved the weather. He chose to come across the northern part of the country first because a southern route would have put him in the plains states in the middle of winter, he said, adding that he didn't expect the northern states to be easy walks.

But he said he has missed much of the bad weather. Severe cold spells arrived and left the Dakotas and Montana before he arrived and snowstorms last week were closing mountain passes and roads over which he had walked the week before.

"I seem to be walking between rain drops. It's great," he said. "It makes the trip much more pleasant."

Sweetgall flew to Ancorage, Alaska, Saturday, the landing delayed while more than a foot of snow was cleared from the runway. He presented a talk and walking clinic at a sports store Saturday night.

"On Sunday, I walked about 11 miles through Anchorage. It is beautiful, with the mountain ranges in the background," he said.

"It's new, having been rebuilt after earthquakes in the 1960s. It gets light at 10:30 in the morning and dark at 4 p.m. It's also very expensive. A cheese omlet will cost you $7."

Sweetgall returned to Seattle at 5:30 a.m. Monday and started walking again, putting in 33 miles before stopping. He spent New Year's Eve in a truck stop motel in Chehalis. Supper was hot dog rolls and cheese cooked in a microwave. "They had Saturday night bingo on New Year's Eve, a huge supermarket type of building was full of people playing bingo," he said.

He said the effects of the eruption of Mount St. Helens in 1980 are still visible in towns in the area, with the volcanic dust settled between the cracks in the sidewalks.

His loose change collection is $37.02. He found a penny in Anchorage. The only states in which he hasn't found change on the roads are West Virginia and Delaware.

*Jan. 3, 1985* ——————————————— *Week 17*

YONCALLA, Ore. — The aroma of freshly-split wood and the rumble of logging trucks have followed Robert J. Sweetgall on his trek through Oregon lumber country this past week.

"It's been like splitting a tree open and living inside," he said of the area that's been his home since last Wednesday.

From the minute Sweetgall crossed the border from Washington into Oregon — leaving Rainer, Wash. and industrial pollution behind him — he said the roads have been lined with tall evergreens and mountains.

Sweetgall said he couldn't have asked for better weather. Not only has he continued to miss major storms, but he hasn't seen more than "Oregon mist" — mountains melting into gray skies — since Christmas. Temperatures have averaged in the 30s during the day and dipped down to the 20s at night.

Sweetgall has had some trouble this week with meeting his mileage goals. Yesterday, for example, he had planned to be at Rice Hill by 1 p.m. and was still two miles away at that time. Fortunately, he said this has not affected his progress. To date, he has walked 3,770 miles, or one-third of the planned distance on the year-long trip.

Oregon is the 18th state he has visited on the tour.

On the road last Thursday morning he was treated to a view of snow-covered Mount St. Helens, which is in Washington State. He described it as "peaceful and serene" despite reports of possible new volcanic activity.

Saturday he walked on to Brooks where he picked up bread and raisins at a local grocery store for breakfast. He said he was very lucky. The store had been robbed the night before.

"People are always asking if I get harassed and here was a near miss," he said. The only thing of note that happened in Salem, Ore., which he reached that day, was having a storeowner refuse to let him use the restroom. Sweetgall admitted he hadn't showered for several days.

Saturday night he slept in Albany and made it to the Hiway Honker restaurant in Tangent for breakfast Sunday morning. Pastor Staub of the Church of God rescued Sweetgall Sunday night when he arrived in the town of Harrisburg and found out there were no motels. The pastor let him sleep on the church floor.

He made Junction City Monday morning where he spoke at the Oaklea Middle School, which he called "one of finest schools in the country" because of its emphasis on health and physical fitness. Sweetgall said all the major network affililates covered the talk. That night, in a suburb of Eugene, he stayed with the family of Dave Wilcox, former player for the San Francisco '49ers football team and now a seed farmer and health spa entrepreneur.

From Eugene he walked through a series of small towns along old Route 99, which winds through forests, horse ranches and small farms. Sweetgall said Cindy, a waitress at a truck stop in Curtain, Ore., remembered him from his last trip and put in his order of spaghetti with melted cheese, without asking.

His loose change total was $41.16.

— AMY ZUCEKRMAN

*Jan. 10, 1985* —————————————— *Week 18*

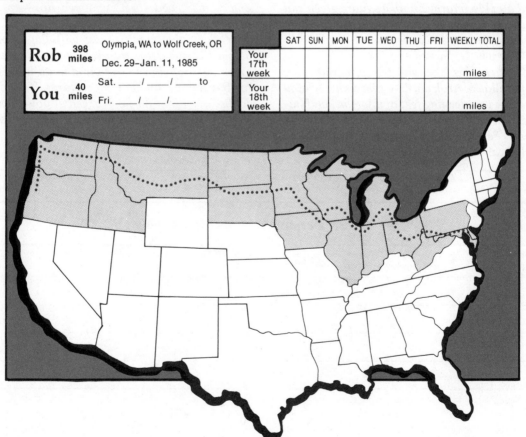

## 17  The Secret of Bag Balm

On a cold winter night on my first trek of America, I limped into the wheat-farming town of Waterville, Washington (pop. 800) on a 10-day old puffy blister that I had been wearing since Kelso, Washington. From the Dodge House cafe, I dialed the telephone number of a dentist that a principal had given me up the road. One-half hour later, Dr. John Rudd was examining my left foot in front of his family at home. He left the living room and quickly returned with a square green can decorated with a cow's head framed in a wreath of roses. It was Bag Balm.

"Bag who?," I asked.

"Just try this," he said, scooping out some stiff yellow petroleum-like ointment. "I used to dress the bleeding feet of my Alaskan Huskies with this when they raced in slush and snow. Farmers use Bag Balm all the time to help heal cracked, bleeding teats. Great stuff."

That night, I rubbed the cow salve all over my feet before retiring in the Rudd guest room. Dr. Rudd also gave me a vial of it to last me until the next pharmacy. And so day and night, every day thereafter, I applied the balm. By Spokane my feet were smooth, soft and healed.

I've learned this same ointment, once the 1906 homemade recipe of a Vermont pharmacist, has also been used by humans to cure diaper rash, bed sores, chapped lips—even hemorrhoids.

While having great success with Bag Balm at subfreezing temperatures, I experienced excessive foot skin redness and irritation using Bag Balm in higher temperatures. It seems to dissolve the skin. So proceed at your own risk. All the cans I've ever bought said "For Veterinary Use Only."

## 18  Your Personal Foot Notes

# Land of Lumber, Rice and Nuts

Photo by David Parker, Marysville Appeal Democrat.

**The Long Stretches**   Old Highway 99 in the Sacramento Valley is right on the migration path of the Canadian Honkers. Rice farmers have turned their paddies into profitable hunting territories by flooding the land to attract geese. Much of the highway runs alongside nut orchards, too. A vegetarian can do pretty well foraging for almonds and English walnuts along these back roads.

# Good-by Oregon, Hello California

DUNSMUIR, Calif. — "There is no southern California. There's no such thing," 28-year-old Derrick told Robert Sweetgall. "It's really a corporate ladder climb where everyone is living for status and possessions.

"Northern California is where people come to get away from it all," the former circus handyman and teepee dweller, now groundskeeper at the Swallow Tavern and Cafe in Hilt told Sweetgall.

Sweetgall Monday crossed into northern California at Hilt, a town of 20 people and a 30-foot statue of Buddah. Sweetgall, who quit a $50,000 a year chemical engineering job to promote health and physical fitness, said he could understand Derrick's feelings about southern California.

This is the most picturesque part of the trip so far," Sweetgall said. "'I'm walking in a canyon between mountain ranges. At the edge of the road along the Klamath River there is a drop of about 1,000 feet. No guardrails. The road is completely up and down — up 1,000 feet, down 1,000 feet — like a roller coaster. It's tough on the legs and it never ends.

"This morning I was walking at 4:15 a.m. and the sunrise was a pink cotton candy clouded sky, the crescent moon lighting up the canyon rocks." Asked why he was walking so early he replied, "I had to get to school on time" (he spoke at 9 a.m. yesterday at Weed Elementary School).

"I've looked at Mount Shasta (elevation 14,162 feet) for two days now, and it doesn't look as if I've gotten any closer. It is a huge mound of earth. In darkness, you can see the sun reflecting off the snow-covered peaks.

Sweetgall has walked 4,001 miles since leaving Newark, Del., on Sept 7. He said the weather here continues to be unseasonably dry, with temperatures in the 20s mornings and 40s afternoons. He said because of late starts, engagements at schools and interviews, he has been walking in the dark most days.

In Roseburg, Ore., last Thursday, he finally decided to stop wearing reflection stripes on his suit because drivers "have been putting their highbeams on me and seeing how close they can get to me. It's too dangerous."

Tired of the interstate with its "truck stops, traffic and milemarkers that tell you how far you've gone and remind you how far you have to go," he stepped off the highway onto "Old 99, a scenic, winding, old country road."

At Wolf Creek he stayed in an old restored stagecoach tavern with oak floors, brass beds and a wood stove. Saturday night he stayed at the Gold Hill Hotel.

Sweetgall slept upstairs, directly over the tall speakers used by the loud rock band down below. He fell asleep during a band break.

"Oregon was very nice, but the main complaint the people I talked with had was that the cause of most of the crimes and problems is marijuana growing.

Monday he stayed at the Swallow Tavern in a broken down, unheated trailer. All the other cabins and trailers were rented to fishermen.

His loose change collection is $43.98 to date. At a school assembly last Thursday at the Fir Grove Elementary School he mentioned that he had found more than $40 on ground. At the end of the assembly he noticed three girls looking for money under the chairs.

*Jan. 17, 1985* ——————————— *Week 19*

VERONA, Calif. — The streets are paved with walnuts, and Robert Sweetgall is making good use of them.

He stuffs his pockets with the light brown, meaty nuts to eat as he walks along the winding roads here.

"The nuts are all along the sides of the roads, falling off the trees," he said in a telephone call yesterday. Because of the numbers of drivers who have crashed into the trees, the state has painted the bottom four feet of each tree white so that they will be visible to drivers at night.

Sweetgall has been working his way down the center of the state of California along routes 5, 99 and 113, through towns named Cotton Wood, Red Bluff, Los Molinos, Chico and Live Oak. He expected to arrive in Sacramento today. From there he will head west on Route 80 — with some backroad detours — to San Francisco.

He is in the Sacramento Valley "where descriptions of the towns sound like basketball game scores — population 118, elevation 110. The land is flatter than in any part of the country I've seen so far," he said.

"It's rice patty country, but the rice isn't as important ecnomically as hunting — duck, pheasant, goose. There are hunting and gun clubs everywhere. One club near here has a lifetime membership fee of $37,000, and that just gets you in the door. Then you have to pay other fees.

"The people say its cold here but it's 30 to 40 degrees, which is a little warm for me. There's a fog inversion which is blocking out the sun. A half hour away in the Sierras it's sunny, 60 and people are skiing," Sweetgall said. "When the sun comes out here it will be 55 to 60 degrees."

He said he has not seen rain for 33 days. "At this time of year it should be raining 70 percent of the time," Sweetgall said.

It's 20 to 30 miles between "big" cities with populations of 5,000 to 10,000. "There are a lot of little hamlets. It's not crowded here," he said, "but it's not like Montana either, with 40 miles of absolutely nothing."

Although a day and a half ahead of schedule, Sweetgall said he expected to lose time between here and San Francisco because the roads are longer than he had estimated. "They wind back and forth along the Feather River and are not straight roads," he said. In the past week he has put in two days of 40 plus miles and three days of about 38 miles each.

"Tuesday night I fell asleep walking and almost walked off a 20-foot embankment into a ditch," he said. "I'm a little tired, but physically I'm in good shape."

Sweetgall has walked 4,240 miles so far, 239 miles since last Wednesday.

He said, "People here are friendly, but cautious because of problems involving drugs."

The main topic of conversation the past week was the Super Bowl, Sweetgall said. Sunday night he saw the last minute of the first half in a gas station as he left the college town of Chico. An hour and a half later he walked into a gas station in Dunham and watched the last five minutes of the game.

Sweetgall said his loose change collection now totals $45.55.

*Jan. 24, 1985 ——————————— Week 20*

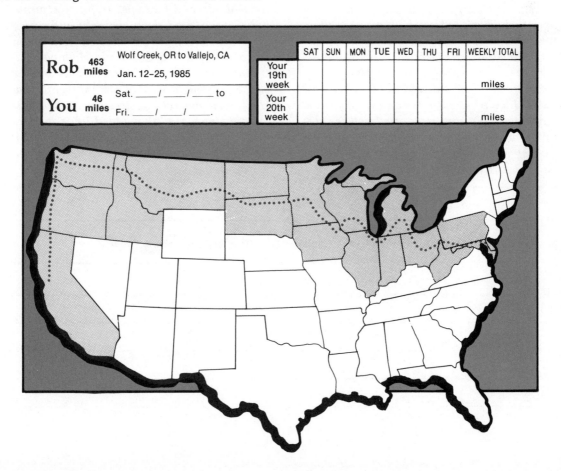

| Rob 463 miles | Wolf Creek, OR to Vallejo, CA Jan. 12–25, 1985 | | SAT | SUN | MON | TUE | WED | THU | FRI | WEEKLY TOTAL |
|---|---|---|---|---|---|---|---|---|---|---|
| You 46 miles | Sat. ___/___/___ to Fri. ___/___/___. | Your 19th week | | | | | | | | miles |
| | | Your 20th week | | | | | | | | miles |

**19** Planning an Eleven-thousand-mile Journey

*In planning a journey involving a detailed speaking itinerary, timing is everything. Schools are waiting for their assemblies. Special events are planned. The road show must go on.*

*So how do you plan it? Deserts, mountains, farmlands, interstates, back roads, big cities, little towns, north first (?), south first (?), . . . how do you pick a route? What time of year do I want to be in the desert? What does that do to the rest of my weather situation? Hence, I studied 50-year weather histories to improve my statistical odds of missing blizzards and severe precipitation.*

*My final route calculated out at 10,900 miles. I added about 6% contingency (road maps generally understate the walker's distance) and came up with 11,600—divided that by 364 (days) to arrive at 32 miles per day. Then I replotted the detailed course—*

*city by city, mile by mile—not worrying about where I'd sleep or eat, just paying close attention to the roads and distances—the numbers—making sure not to slip a digit. The north country (Minnesota through Montana) would be late fall to put me in the Mojave Desert in the dead of winter. The south I would need to walk in summer.*

*Then the time comes when you're out there for real—face to face with traffic, just praying that you read the maps right and added up those thousands of miles without error. All of a sudden, a California Highway Patrolman stops you on the freeway, as was the case Friday night west of Dixon, California. He forced me off the freeway onto some winding back road that added 10 or so extra miles to my already tight schedule. So that night I walked until midnight to find a motel. What else can you do?*

---

**20** **Your Personal Foot Notes**

---

# The Pacific

**Walking on Water to Hawaii**
You can't do a 50-state walk without touching Hawaii. So I flew there, and then walked. From the airport I headed downtown and visited the old market and fishing wharf. Lunch was white rice ala foot bath in the Pacific. By evening I was walking back in a thunderstorm to catch my 8 P.M. plane. For the day I racked up 20 miles, 77¢ in loose change, no taxis, 1 school lecture—not exactly your average Hawaiian tour package.

Photo by Honolulu Star Bulletin.

# Tough Times with the California Highway Patrol

PALO ALTO, Calif. — In the span of four days, Robert Sweetgall got thrown off an interstate highway by the Highway Patrol; attended a reception at which Mayor Diane Feinstein proclaimed last Sunday Rob Sweetgall Day in San Francisco and flew to Honolulu where he talked to fifth-graders who consider it a treat to go swimming in a swimming pool.

Sweetgall has walked 205 miles in the past week, some of it unexpected walking because of his banishment from the interstate highways. He said 34 California Highway Patrolmen had passed him without incident until a highway patrolman stopped him outside Sacramento last Thursday night. "He stopped me just on a check. He was fairly friendly. He called his lieutenant to see if I could cross an area where I wasn't supposed to cross," Sweetgall said.

"He was trying to help, but the lieutenant told me to get off."

That turned a four-mile walk to the nearest motel into a nine-mile walk.

Friday he got lost twice and spent the day walking underpasses and overpasses back roads, residential streets and old highways in an attempt to get to San Francisco without going on the interstate. He said, "I walked about 25 miles Friday but I only advanced half that distance."

At a truck stop Friday night he saw the highway patrolman who first stopped him Thursday. Sweetgall said, "He apologized for what happened, and told me he thought he was being helpful. He then spent an hour and a half showing me the back roads to an old highway into Vallejo. He saved me about six miles of extra walking.

"Sunday was (spent) walking through Sausalito to San Francisco, by yacht basins, piers, bluffs overlooking San Francisco, over the Golden Gate Bridge, thousands of homes lining the ocean, blue-green sparkling waters, Chinatown, the different ethnic areas, outdoor market places, trolley tracks, up and down the hills . . ."

On Monday he flew to Honolulu. He said, "I felt like half a mule and half a walker I had so much clothing on — three layers of woolen clothes and it was 80 degrees and sunny."

He got off the plane and began walking downtown. He saw a sign that said Puuhale (pronounced Poo-oo-holly) Elementary School, located across from the state prison. He went in and asked the principal if he could talk to the students about walking and health.

"When I walked in, the principal, Shirley Miyamota, was reprimanding a student for starting a fire. The school had burned down 20 years ago and when rebuilt became the only school in Hawaii with air conditioning and soundproofing (because of the nearness of the airport)," he said.

Sweetgall said the fifth-grade students' favorite foods are pizza and French fries, that they prefer swimming in a swimming pool to swimming in the ocean and that they can't imagine any weather colder than 60 degrees.

After presenting a program at the school, he walked 15 miles into downtown Honolulu. "It was a little like the old marketplace in Philadelphia along the river. I liked the old section, but it also has a lot of gas stations and fast food places. The beaches are nice, but commercialized.

"My feet were hot so I walked to the beach, where I sat on lava rock, bathing my feet in the crystal clear, green water, watching boys race outrigger canoes, the sun setting behind pink clouds over the horizon," he said.

Sweetgall said his loose change collection is now $47.42.

*Jan. 31, 1985* ———————— *Week 21*

SANTA MARIA, Calif. — In the last week Robert Sweetgall has suffered his first blisters in almost 4,200 miles, the result of warmer weather and new shoes; met a man who grew up a few blocks from him in Brooklyn, N.Y., and aided weary walkers reenacting a Civil War event.

"I developed blood blisters on the heels last Thursday from too much pounding and heat buildup, plus a new pair of shoes. Usually that type of blister is painful and slow healing, but I walked about 85 percent of the last 200 miles without socks and the blisters healed in two days," he said.

He said the lack of blisters has been "primarily due to a high degree of dedicated foot maintenance, including the use of balms, moisturizers and ointments and airing the feet whenever I get a chance."

Sweetgall has walked a total of 4,710 miles — 265 miles of that in the past week. He said he has been getting off the road about 11:30 each night, a very late hour, but necessary because he's trying to make Castaic on Friday for a school assembly.

His biggest mileage day was Sunday, when he walked 59 miles. Finding no lodging in Bradley, he headed for San Miguel, 14 miles away. He said, "It's a tough town; a lot of robberies, fights. Not the kind of place where I wanted to go knocking on doors looking for a place to stay."

At 3 a.m. he found the Mission Motel, signed the register "A.M. Tired from Sleepy Hollow" and was in bed at 3:09. He said, "The next morning I sat in a restaurant eating a bowl of spaghetti while a man with two teeth sat next to me describing a big bar brawl in town a few months back."

Last Wednesday, he met Mike DeClemente, who recognized Sweetgall from a television news program, as Sweetgall walked by a shopping mall. DeClemente, a bus driver, gave up his car last year when it broke down on the way to the airport. "He started riding a bike, but he crashed. He said riding a bike out here is like swimming with sharks. Now he walks everywhere he goes. He walked about seven miles with me," Sweetgall said.

Sweetgall learned the bus driver grew up a few blocks from where Sweetgall was raised in South Flatbush, Brooklyn, and that his relatives live a block away from Sweetgall's mother.

On Friday, he met four men who were reenacting the march of Union soldiers 120 years ago from San Jose in San Juan Bautista. They were wearing reproductions of Civil War army uniforms, including shoes, and were on the second day of a three-day, 40-mile march. They had some painful blisters, so Sweetgall ministered their wounds and gave them some lotions and advice on airing their feet.

He had planned to make Santa Barbara last night, turning east today to walk through forest and mountains as he heads west to Santa Paula, Filmore and across to Nevada. He said he expected to be in California for another week.

His loose change collection is now $52.45.

*Feb. 7, 1985* ————————————— *Week 22*

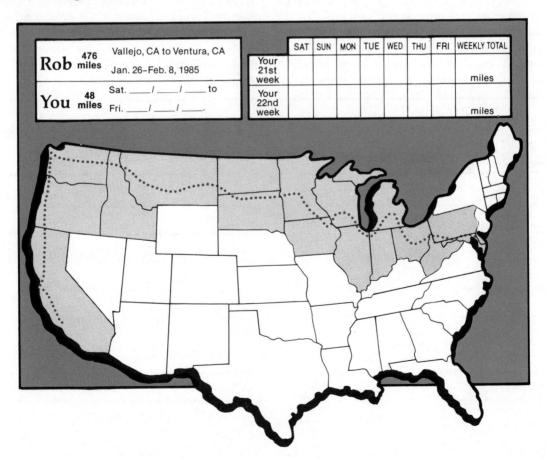

# Foot Notes      Weeks 21 & 22

### 21   Risk Taking

*For weeks on the phone during my walk, I'd been trying to sell a free school assembly to Hawaiian administrators. All I wanted was to conduct one educational program in Hawaii. "Rob Sweetgall who?," was a typical response. After about $20 of these calls, I said "forget it." But the urge came back the morning I arrived in Honolulu. The first school that I passed on Nimitz Boulevard, I entered. At first Principal Shirley Miyamota didn't know what to say—a guy looking like a Montana prospector in heavy-duty winter gear drops in, displays a few news articles for an I.D., and then asks to talk to her students on "health." Risky? Well, finally she consented, and we had a nice, educational show for her 4th and 5th-grade classes. Everyone was delighted.*

*Looking back on my journey, the whole thing was a big risk—crazy people on the road, drunken drivers, physical and mental breakdowns—you name it. Maybe that's why my most rewarding road experiences came when a total stranger trusted me at the front door, purely on faith. One boy, a chef out of Canyon Country, California, had an interesting way of looking at it: "I can't turn a stranger down," he said. "You never know when God's sending angels down to Earth in disguise."*

### 22   Your Personal Foot Notes

_____

_____

_____

_____

_____

_____

_____

_____

# The Mojave Desert

**Yucca Lunch**  It's tough to buy food in the desert—especially if you are a vegetarian. Here in the thin shade of a Yucca plant in the Great Basin, I'm living off a 24-slice loaf of whole wheat bread which I've compressed into a softball for ease of transport. Lunch is 3 tears off the softball. Snacks are 1 tear—about 65 calories—of which 50% by weight is water. At the next highway casino store I'll buy a fresh softball.

Photo John Malmin, Los Angeles Times.

# In February, Mojave Rattlesnakes Sleep

VICTORVILLE, CALIF. — Robert Sweetgall walks while the rattlesnakes sleep.

"I planned to be in the desert in the winter because I knew that if I tried to walk it in the summer either the weather would kill me or the rattlesnakes would," Sweetgall said in a telephone call yesterday from the Mojave Desert.

"But the rattlesnakes sleep this time of year. They are on the rocks and they're not moving. It's the only time of year that they are dormant.

Even though it is winter here, the desert is the hardest part of the walk, Sweetgall said. "It's overpowering in its vastness. It's beautiful when its losing or gaining its colors at sunrise and sunset, but it's ugly during the daylight hours. All I see during the day is Joshua and Yucca trees, sage brush, sand and broken asphalt. The towns are 25 to 40 miles apart," he said.

Sweetgall has walked a total of 4,925 miles, 215 since last Thursday. He will spend the next three days walking through the California desert before crossing into Nevada Sunday, putting in 16 hour days, walking from 5 a.m. to 9 p.m. each day.

"The desert is very hard physically. I have to look for garbage bags or cartons to sit down on so I don't get bitten by the scorpions and red ants and other things in the sand when I take care of my feet," he said.

The roads are two lanes with no shoulder except the sand, rocks and sage brush. "You've got to think every minute where you're stepping. It's easy to turn an ankle and the traffic is always within one foot of you. When the semis come I either have to make them move over a foot or I jump into sage brush and dust. I jump a lot," Sweetgall said.

In some ways, he said, Southern California has been tough mentally — depressing him despite its beauty. He's found the lifestyle upsetting. "People in places like Santa Barbara, Los Angeles, or the little yuppie communities around Southern California are really into themselves. They deal in high fences and double deadbolt doors," he said.

"The desert has a reputation and peoples' attitudes reflect it," Sweetgall said. "There's a certain desperateness you feel. It's not the kind you feel in a blizzard. It's a whole different attitude. It was 'Howdy, partner,' in Dakota and Montana and Washington. Out here it's 'Sorry, stranger'."

But Sweetgall said there are kind, helpful people, too. Edna and Phil Billings, owners of a motel in Carpinteria, Friday drove Sweetgall to a school program in Castaic, 60 miles away, and back agiain. They refused the $60 he offered.

Saturday the trip turned east for the first time in five months, walking through orchards of lemons and oranges and avocadoes. ("The penalty for picking avocadoes up off the ground is $500 for the first offense — that's because you could make a living out here just stealing avocadoes").

His loose change collection is $59.76. "There's a lot of money in the desert."

*Feb. 14, 1985* —————————————— *Week 23*

LAS VEGAS — Robert Sweetgall expected to walk down the glittering neon strip here last night after returning east for his periodic medical tests, but today he will be back under the glare of the desert sun.

Although Sweetgall has had no major problems, he has been troubled recently by sore feet and temperatures soaring into the 80s as he crossed the Mojave Desert. He said he is spending about three hours each day on foot care, stopping every 40 minutes to treat his feet with rubbing alcohol and moisturizers.

The toughest part is ahead of him, he said, as he faces 300 more miles of desert with three cities 75 miles apart and no small towns in between. He said he will have to arrange for someone to pick him up at night and take him to the nearest city, returning him to the highway in the morning.

To keep himself occupied while walking, Sweetgall said he played "mind games." The game he has been playing most often he calls Recall, during which he remembers past experiences, people, places or events. "Right now I can recall every single day of the trip," he said.

He also dictates his feelings and observations into a microcassette recorder, sightsees, does mathematics problems or makes plans. He said, "There are so many things to think about that it never gets boring."

"In the desert you can see for 20 miles," Sweetgall said during tests at the medical center yesterday. "The highway looks like a piece of chocolate carpet running up the hills. The cars seem to be hardly moving because you can see them coming from so far away." He said Highway 15, which he has been walking on, is a busy road, with 5,000-10,000 cars an hour passing him.

Last Thursday, he spoke to about 300 students in Barstow, a city of truck stops, gas stations and motels, located at the junction of routes 40 and 15.

"A fourth-grader asked me a question I hadn't heard before. She wanted to know how I knew where I had stopped walking the day before if someone had to take me back to the highway. I told her I either marked a spot on the gravel at the side of the road or tied a dirty sock to a post," he said.

Friday night he slept at a Chevron gas station off the highway, about 12 miles short of Baker. "Three brothers own the station. They let me sleep in a Pontiac Catalina station wagon with 130,000 miles, a blown engine and a dusty back seat," he said.

He crossed into Nevada Sunday, the countryside "looking like the outfield in old Yankee Stadium, it was plastered with billboards — 'Shake, Rattle and Roll.' There are slot machines everywhere, restaurants, truck stops.

Shortly before the "Welcome to Silver State" sign at the Nevada border on Sunday, Sweetgall found 30 nickles and two quarters, most new and shiny, gleaming on the black asphalt. "Maybe they fell out of a slot machine on the back of a pickup truck," he said.

His loose change total is now $62.10.

*Feb. 21, 1985* ——————————— *Week 24*

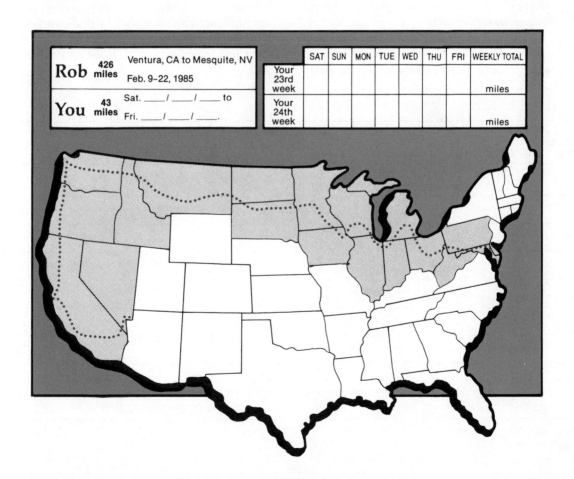

| | SAT | SUN | MON | TUE | WED | THU | FRI | WEEKLY TOTAL |
|---|---|---|---|---|---|---|---|---|
| Your 23rd week | | | | | | | | miles |
| Your 24th week | | | | | | | | miles |

**Rob** 426 miles — Ventura, CA to Mesquite, NV — Feb. 9–22, 1985

**You** 43 miles — Sat. ___/___/___ to Fri. ___/___/___.

## 23 | Talking Mailboxes

I don't usually talk to mailboxes, except when the dirt driveways on the prairie are 1 or 2 miles long, and I need a favor at a rancher's door. Then it helps to talk to the driveway butler—the mailbox—before making that long, dusty approach. A mailbox decorated with humor is a good omen—a friendly spot to hit. One with conventional Sears-Roebuck stick-on black letters . . . hummm, I think I'll pass. Driveway dogs also speak for their masters. Beware.

On a cold Sunday west of Mobridge, I was walking Highway 12 west across the Sioux Indian Reservation, looking for a wind-brake shelter to rest off the road. Straight ahead I saw the perfect invitation—a driveway mailbox mounted on a stainless steel toilet bowl that doubled as a flower holder. The toilet was the kind I've seen in several jail cells. At the back door, an Indian man answered my knock. Minutes later he was slicing up oranges for me in the dining room.

One day, limping along in the Mojave, I thought of my old Sioux Indian friend everytime I passed a desert house guarded by prison-type barbed wire fence and barking canines. One house had a sign, "Trespassers will be shot!"

## 24 | Your Personal Foot Notes

# Great Basin & Painted Deserts

Photo by John Malmin, Los Angeles Times.

**Thin Company**   North of Las Vegas, Highway 93 runs along gravel pits, gulches, and sandstone mesas. The Sheep and Mormon Mountains surround the Great Basin. Often I'd walk for hours and not see a soul. At the junction of 93 and I-15 was a man dressed in green army fatigues pushing a supermarket cart filled with a sleeping bag, blanket, overcoat, and junk. From across the road I called to him, "How far ya goin'?" He removed the unlit cigarette from his mouth and responded, "What are you, one of those nosybodies with all your questions?"

# Halfway Home—Sandstone River Canyons

KANAB, Utah — "You could just live for the fiery, orange-red sunsets each day. And the sunrises... the land changes color as the sun comes up on the sandstone mountains and the bright red rocks turn pink to coral to beige. It's the prettiest area of country so far."

Robert Sweetgall nipped the northwest corner of Arizona Saturday and yesterday was on the southern edge of Utah, walking through the Great Basin Desert, a dry, peaceful land of great beauty.

"There are occasional jack rabbits, a little grass and a few thin-looking cows," he said.

"From a distance, the tops of the sage brush and Joshua trees give the mistaken impression of green fields."

But it was the gorges cut by wind and water from sandstone that could take away one's breath, Sweetgall said. He spoke of the miniature grand canyons, jagged cliffs, mesas that looked like flattop haircuts — a land cut from the sand.

"Except for Alaska, this is probably the remotest part of the United States I will visit," he said.

Sweetgall was in his 23rd state and has walked 5,355 miles, 235 miles in the past week. Except for medical tests in Worcester Feb. 19, he has spent the last 14 days and 500 miles crossing desert.

"There has been no rain. It's cold in the morning, 25 degrees, and warm in the afternoon, 50-55," he said, "clear skies, a little wind."

Towns are about 30 miles apart, so Sweetgall now buys a loaf of whole wheat bread, rolls it into a softball-size shape and stuffs it in his winter mitten. In the other mitten he carries a 16-ounce bottle of soda. It is the most food he has carried and the only food he carries into the desert.

At times when he has found himself in the desert at night he has had to rely on rides to the nearest town for the night and rides back the next day to pick up where he left off.

"The people are much friendlier here than in the Mojave Desert on the other side of Las Vegas," he said.

Saturday morning he crossed into Arizona. "The Virgin River there is just a 20-foot-wide stream of muck and mud, but it is responsible for tremendous gorges. The river has cut these 300-400 foot high gorges out of the sandstone and lava arock. For about five or six miles I walked through this tremendous rock corridor with the wind whistling and the sand changing color, depending on the sun.

"The trees are starting to show signs of spring, the cedar and cottonwoods. There are a lot of sandstone homes, primarily brick red, made of compressed layers of sand that have been cut from the hills. They make guardrails out of it, too," Sweetgall said.

Monday he began his walk through the Zion National Park. "That had to be one of the scenic highlights of the tour. It looked like I expected the Grand Canyon to look, only smaller, but better I think because you're part of the canyon, you can walk through it," Sweetgall said.

Sweetgall said his loose change collection now totals $65.05.

*Feb. 28, 1985* ———————————— *Week 25*

WINONA, Ariz. — Robert Sweetgall finishes the first half of his year-long trip tonight in Winslow, completing his 26th week on the road.

Since he left Newark, Del., Sept. 7, he has walked 5,580 miles (close to the halfway point in mileage, too), averaging 31 miles a day, through 1,000 cities and towns; spoken to 15,000 people at 71 events, including school assemblies, and had about 150 interviews, including television, radio and newspapers and magazines.

About 800 children and adults have walked at least a half mile with him during the walk. Two North Dakota farmers joined him for 101 miles.

Yesterday he continued his trip through the desert, alone, carrying only his five-pound waist pack, a loaf of wheat bread and bottle of soda.

He again is wearing his first — and favorite — pair of shoes, which are now 2,500 miles old.

"So far the walk has been very successful. It has been essentially injury-free," except for 11 blisters, most at the beginning of the walk, and a dry, cracked left heel that has caused him to limp slightly the last 100 miles.

"The biggest shock has been the weather. I've had fewer than 10 hours of rain in the last 70 days, starting in the Pacific northwest," he said.

Cities and towns are few and far between "although there is a trading post about every 20 miles, an occasional dog or two patrolling a herd of goats or sheep. It's still desert, but there are a lot of ridges. It's like walking through the Grand Canyon."

Most of the past week has been spent walking through the Navajo Indian reservation. He said, "Every half mile you will find an Indian home tucked back into the foothills of cliffs. They're called hogans, little sandstone huts shaped like an octagon with the door facing east. They have dirt floors and 55-gallon drums for stoves.

"Basically, I'm walking on the floor of an ocean that was here 10 million years ago, before the Sierra Nevadas erupted with lava, pushing mountains up," he said.

"It is compressed layers of sand and on the ridges you can see beige, yellow, orange, red and green. It's very pretty here, the Painted Desert with its different colors of sandstone."

The land here is high, with Flagstaff's 7,000-foot elevation the highest on the tour. McDonald's Pass at the Continental Divide is 6,325 feet, "but you come back down. The elevation is a problem, and adjusting from 6,000 feet in one place to 6,500 feet the next day makes me dizzy, weak and short of breath. Unfortunately, by the time I become acclimated to it, I've moved on to another elevation," he said.

The weather has been cool and windy and he has had to eat dust at times as the 40-mile-an-hour winds blew the sand at him. The heat varies with the altitude, from 0 degrees to 25 degrees in the morning and up to 55 degrees in the afternoon.

He has found $66.10 along the roads for his "loose change" collection during the first half of his journey, a figure he said surprised him. "I don't think that will keep up," he said.

*March 7, 1985* ——————————— *Week 26*

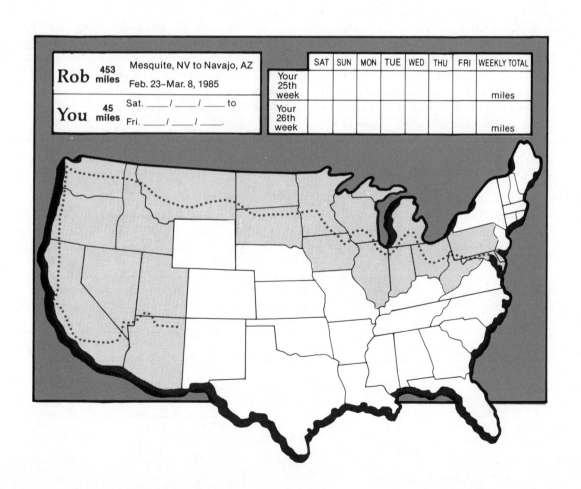

| | | | | | | | | | |
|---|---|---|---|---|---|---|---|---|---|
| **Rob** 453 miles | Mesquite, NV to Navajo, AZ  Feb. 23–Mar. 8, 1985 | | SAT | SUN | MON | TUE | WED | THU | FRI | WEEKLY TOTAL |
| **You** 45 miles | Sat. ___/___/___ to  Fri. ___/___/___. | | Your 25th week | | | | | | | | miles |
| | | | Your 26th week | | | | | | | | miles |

### 25 Loneliness

*Loneliness was a recurring but brief state of mind throughout the trek. It came most often in the pre-sunrise hours when I stepped out into the black air. The degree of loneliness often depended on how attached I became to new friend(s) the evening before. Most often "it" dissolved with the first rays of the morning sun on the horizon. By then, I was usually on my way to making a new friend—a waitress, a grocer, a motorist stopping to chat, a child going to school, or a neighborhood dog looking for a little companionship.*

*On the road you learn to become your own companion—for better or for worse—like during all those hundreds of miles of deserts and prairies and telephone poles when sometimes I'd walk for 20 miles alone. Then I'd call on my memory to bring back an interesting road acquaintance. Using imagery, I'd place him or her right beside me in conversation. I'd recall the gestures, the clothes, the features, and the talk we had. In vivid detail. Frequently, I'd pull out my tape recorder and listen to past tapes of great conversations while walking. Then the details came back clear. It was just as if that person was at my side.*

*On this subject, Edward Gibbon wrote, "On the approach of spring I withdraw without reluctance from the noisy and extensive scene of crowds without company, and dissipation with pleasure. . . . I was never less alone than when by myself."*

### 26 Your Personal Foot Notes

_____

_____

_____

_____

_____

_____

_____

# The Santa Fe Trail

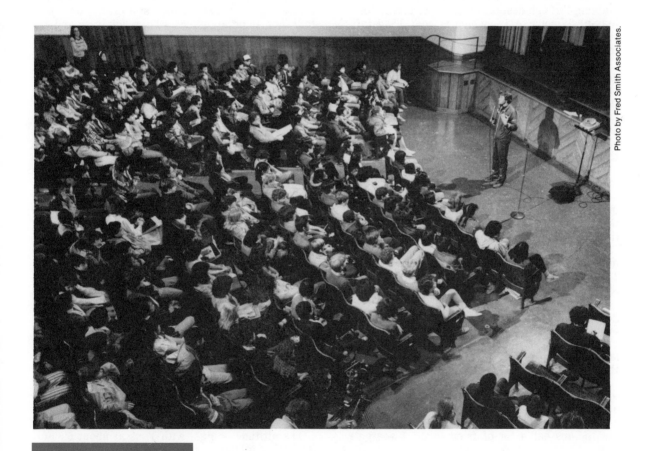

Photo by Fred Smith Associates.

**Walk-in School Assemblies**
Elementary school kids make the best audiences. They are attentive, and they absorb. You just know your message is getting through. A good impression can last a child a lifetime. During my school assemblies on tour, children ask plenty of questions about "life on the road." But they also want to know things like: "Will their parents' tobacco smoke hurt their bodies?"

53

# Passing Through Spanish History

GRANTS, N. MEX. — By next week Robert J. Sweetgall will have walked through 25 states — half of his goal.

This week he has been nursing a sore left heel that has "fluctuated from better to worse."

In a telephone interview yesterday Sweetgall said, "There's a crack in the heel. It heals then splits, then heals and splits. It's been giving me a rough time. I just wish it would heal completely."

Since last Wednesday Sweetgall has been walking through desert and prairie ranges. Since leaving Winona, Ariz., which is near Flagstaff, the altitude has been dropping steadily from more than 7,000 ft. to 6,000 to 5,000 ft.

Sweetgall got into Winslow, Ariz. on Thursday night. "That day was basically just walking with one cafe stop in the prairie. The place was about the size of a shoebox.

The next day he stopped in Joseph City to give a talk.

"The town's about 70 percent Mormon. While talking to the kids, I told them how I sometimes I can't make it to the schools on time. So I have to shuttle in and out.

"One of them asked when I'd be actually walking through Joseph City. I said about 5 p.m. So when I reached the edge of town four kids and their parents were waiting for me," he said.

"They walked the four miles into town with me, where about a dozen adults and kids met me. They were really sorry to leave me when I had to get on the interstate."

Sweetgall stopped that night in Holbrook and gave a talk the next day at Holbrook Junior High School.

He also spoke at Puerco Junior High School later in the day. The population of the town of Puerco is about 90 percent Navajo.

"The Navajos are quiet, people, shy. It's tough to gauge their response. They don't ask too many questions. But this group asked a lot about diet — how to eat less fried, greasy food. I've found the Indians eat a lot of fried food," Sweetgall said.

Sweetgall has been walking through the Painted Desert. But he says from what he's seen there's not much color. "It just looks green with sage brush and sand," he said.

He said walking at night is "pretty peaceful." But he has had to deal with some local supersti-

tions. The most popular of them concerns the "Skin Walker" reported to be a black furry wolf-like phantom, who walks on two legs, at a speed of up to 40 miles an hour.

"A couple had seen it run alongside their car at 40 miles an hour. People here feel it's an evil spirit. It has been sighted a lot in the area," he said.

Sunday night he reached Gallup, the "Navajo Indian Center" of New Mexico.

"Crass commercialism is what it is. There are 32 trading posts selling arts and crafts, 60 restaurants, 40 or so motels, a big truck town and a real turn off for me. I just walked right through on Monday."

He picked up $1.30 in loose change this week, bringing his total to $67.40.

— CHRISTINE R. DUNPHY

*March 14, 1985* ——————— *Week 27*

TAOS, N.M. — The straw sticks out of the mud walls. The apartments are "little cubes, little garden apartments" reached by ladder from the level below. There's no running water, no electricity.

It's the oldest apartment complex in America," Robert Sweetgall said of the Pueblo Village of Taos. "Some parts are open to the public, but Indians still live there the way they did 400 years ago."

New Mexico is a land of living history. Sweetgall said. "The old town squares still have their 15th, 16th century Spanish look. At Tesuque Pueblo, just outside Santa Fe, is the old plaza and the Governor's Hall, two of the oldest public buildings in America."

The roads have been a problem. "About the only thing paved here is the main highway. There are classy homes on unpaved, red earth roads. There are hardly any sidewalks or even place to walk.

The altitude is high, with Taos at about 6,800 feet. It's a a land of mountains, canyons, gorges, mesas and steep rock ledges. Vegetation ranges from sage brush to cedar to Canadian pine and douglas fir. "Sometimes I find myself walking up into grey snow clouds," he said.

Sweetgall broke the 6,000-mile mark Tuesday and has now walked 6,040 miles, 250 miles in the past week. He said he expected to reach Colorado this weekend.

Yesterday he planned to walk from Taos to Eagles Nest, a ski town of about 500 people. The walk would be a change of about 2,000 feet, a big change in one day. "I'll be at about 8,600-9,000 feet at Eagles Nest, the highest altitude I've been," he said.

Sleeping accomodations have been uncertain, with few motels in the small towns. Last Wednesday, he stayed with Floyd Solomon and his family in Laguna. Solomon, an Indian who teaches at a reservation school, "told me he had an offer I couldn't refuse," Sweetgall said. "He said I could get my clothes washed at his house." At Bernadillo, the police let him sleep Friday night in the San Doval County jail holding cell, a converted shower. "They didn't want to put me in a cell because they had 17 prisoners in the four cells. It's a tough town. I should have known that. The first sign I saw when I walked into town was "Bail Bonds — 24 Hours.""

On Tuesday, he slept in an old trailer behind the Downstream Deli near San Juan Pueblo. While in the deli, Sweetgall heard a commotion outside. He and the owners found three large, black pigs eating flowers and peering in the screen door.

"The owner chased them away and a little while later we heard a large thump, as if someone had dropped a 500-pound bag of flour. One of the pigs had been hit at the white stripe on the highway where I had been walking a little earlier," he said.

In New Mexico, it has rained or snowed 70 percent of the time. Tuesday, freezing rain turned to driving snow for about 14 miles.

His loose change colleciton is $70.28, but all the riches are not silver. Thursday on Route 66 he found a nylon baseball jacket, two wrenches, a half-full bottle of skin lotion, a Kennedy half dollar, prescription eyeglasses and a deed to proerty in Missouri, which he mailed to the owner.

*March 21, 1985* ———————— *Week 28*

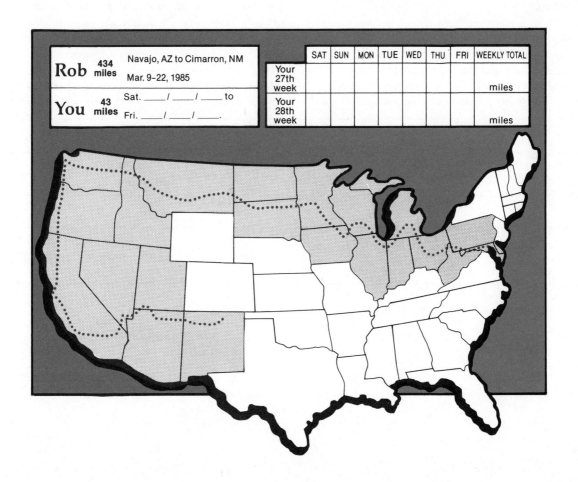

| Rob 434 miles — Navajo, AZ to Cimarron, NM — Mar. 9–22, 1985 | | SAT | SUN | MON | TUE | WED | THU | FRI | WEEKLY TOTAL |
|---|---|---|---|---|---|---|---|---|---|
| You 43 miles — Sat. ___ / ___ / ___ to Fri. ___ / ___ / ___. | Your 27th week | | | | | | | | miles |
| | Your 28th week | | | | | | | | miles |

**27** **Why Should Children Walk?**

*A great many school children today dislike running, and for two good reasons. It's painful and unenjoyable. Yet many school programs encourage children to run. Often kids' fitness levels are measured via running tests—tests in which students are doing poorly. It's easy to blame the student, but did anyone consider that most children simply do not care to run? What are we forcing on them?*

*Now if running were the only road to fitness, it might be another story. But it's not. Consider brisk walking. It has these advantages: (1) Walking can provide the same aerobic benefits as running, yet without pounding the body. (2) Many students get sharp, side abdominal pains (termed "side stitches") from running, but rarely from walking. (3) Children's sweat glands and cooling systems cannot handle high-intensity distance running. (4) A child can walk a mile in 18 minutes, burn 70 calories, feel good—and receive an aerobic conditioning effect at the same time. (5) Walking favors neither sex. (6) Walking requires no special athletic ability. (7) Walking burns fat in obese children. (8) Walking fits into everyday lifestyle with parental involvement. (9) Walking encourages long-term, noncompetitive exercise—not short-term, win-lose burnout. (10) Teachers, parents and students can walk together and communicate. I really like the 10th reason.*

**28** **Your Personal Foot Notes**

# Rocky Mountains

**A Mile High in Slush**
Crossing America, I learned to
live with the weather. This
day—#205 of the walk—was a
21-miler in soupy slush as a
spring snowstorm hit out of the
Rockies dumping 16 inches
worth on Colorado Springs.
Larry Brown and John
Gordon, reporter and
photographer for the Rocky
Mountain News, drove 60
miles through the storm to see
how I was handling the wet
powder.

Photo by John Gordon.

57

# Red Dust, White Snow & Gray Slush

PUEBLO, Colo. — The wind was blowing east "right toward New York City."

Robert Sweetgall was headed north toward Denver.

The two met on Interstate 25. "The wind was blowing so hard I had to walk northwest to get north. Visibility was 10 to 30 feet. Hard walking. It's like when someone's pushing you to go faster and you don't want to go faster. The legs really take a beating, especially when I'm going downhill," he said.

"All I needed was a cape and roller skates."

He crossed from New Mexico to Colorado Sunday, but said he doesn't consider himself out of the desert. "As long as I'm walking on roads on which I can see 15 miles straight ahead and see wide open spaces and sage brush and yucca trees . . . then I still consider it desert," he said. "Actually, it is desert prairie."

The changes in the land in the past week have been impressive, from the desert sands to the mountains of New Mexico to the plains. Last Wednesday he walked the long, winding, uphill road from Taos to Eagle Nest, N.M., 8,900 feet into the mountains, a height that left him short of breath.

"It was an icy, narrow, two-lane road with hairpin turns and little room for error. I had to concentrate on every footstep," he said.

Sweetgall walked through Cimarron Canyon Thursday. "The mist rises from the river gorge, and the road winds along the river. It's mostly tall evergreens and looks something like Montana. There are grey, igneous rock, formations shaped like icicles, 40-million-year-old rock formations with an evergreen covering," he said.

"No civilization. All you can hear is the sound of the river.

"And the vehicles, mostly vans, campers and motor homes with Texas plates.

"On the outskirts of Cimarron I could look back and see the Rocky Mountains and look ahead and see for 50 miles, picturing Kansas and Nebraska out ahead. I felt like I could see America.

"I saw a herd of antelope run away from me at probably 60 miles an hour. I thought they were white tailed deer until someone told me what they were. They can outrun the wind."

At a small cafe on Main Street in Walsenburg at 7:30 Monday morning waitress Tilly Valdez suggested Sweetgall might want to stay in town until about 10 a.m. "I though maybe there was a special event, a parade or something, so I asked her why. 'That's when the Sisters open the used clothes store,' she told me. 'Maybe you can get a newer pair of shoes.'

Sweetgall is wearing the shoes with which he started the trip (They have 3,700 miles on them; have been resoled and have been slit on the sides to let air get to his feet).

Tuesday afternoon he stopped at the farm owned by Victor and Helen Ferrandillo to ask directions and was invited to dinner. After dinner, Ferrandillo and his daughter Crystal, 5, walked across Ferrandillo's cattle range to an old highway leading to Walsenburg. "I felt a nip at my shoulder and turned around to find seven of Ferrandillo's quarter horses walking with us."

The temperature has been 50 to 60 degrees during the day, but weather changes come swiftly. "At 3 Tuesday afternoon it was 60 degrees and sunny. At 3:45 little snowballs about the size of marbles were falling out of the sky. They call it rain here," he said. "I call it snow."

Sweetgall said he found a practically new bicycle seat which he left on the exit 64 post on Route 25. Two hunting knives he found are being sent to friends. His loose change collection is $71.94.

*March 28, 1985 ———————— Week 29*

LOVELAND, Colo. — Colorado has been a disappointment, Robert Sweetgall said — too much of everything except the nature that singer John Denver celebrated in his songs in the 1970s.

"It's not here anymore," Sweetgall said in a telephone call yesterday. "Colorado has lost what Montana is trying to maintain — the natural environment, respect for the environment. People are just strangling themselves out here with overpopulation and pollution."

Sweetgall walked through Colorado Springs late Thursday and early Friday, the second day of a snowstorm that had 30-mile-an-hour winds driving the wet snow at him. The walking was made even more difficult by the inches of slush on the road and snowdrifts up to two feet deep beside the road.

"I was a walking ice man. The slush thrown up by the passing cars would hit and freeze on my walking suit. I couldn't bend my legs because the suit was like paper mache. I couldn't untie my shoes because the laces were frozen," he said.

"Friday night I stayed in a motel on the north side of Colorado Springs. I was so tired I didn't go out, instead finishing a loaf of bread I had bought the day before for dinner. I hung the walking suit over the bathtub and fell asleep listening to the chunks of ice drop off the suit into the tub."

He ran hot water over the shoes to thaw them out then put them in front of a hot air heater to dry them.

Saturday the snow ended, and roads cleared. But the cold temperatures continued. He is walking at an altitude of 5,000 to 6,000 feet. "I'm in the middle of the mountains. To the west are the snow-covered Rockies, about 2,000 to 4,000 feet above me. To the east are rolling hills. But there has been a lot of cloudy weather and the visibility has been poor," he said.

Colorado Gov. Richard Lamm proclaimed yesterday Rob Sweetgall Day. He received a procla-

mation at the state capital then led residents on a short walk through the city.

Sunday afternoon he walked into Denver. "I walked on the bike path. It was strange because Denver has been glorified as a great outdoor metropolis, but I didn't see a single walker and there were only two bikes on the bike path. It was a beautiful sunset, an ideal time for people to be out but there was no one there," he said.

"While walking through downtown I watched the pollution float down the river. The water smells like sewage, and the noise pollution is very bad. Monday morning when I got up I could see the brown cloud of air pollution that hangs over the northern part of the city.

"One man who works testing auto emissions said he sometimes tests the air itself. Sometimes its .05 percent carbon monoxide. Somedays it's .5 percent. 'Someday this is going to kill us,' he told me while he smoked his cigarette."

Sweetgall's loose change collection now totals $73.04.

*April 4, 1985* ———————————— *Week 30*

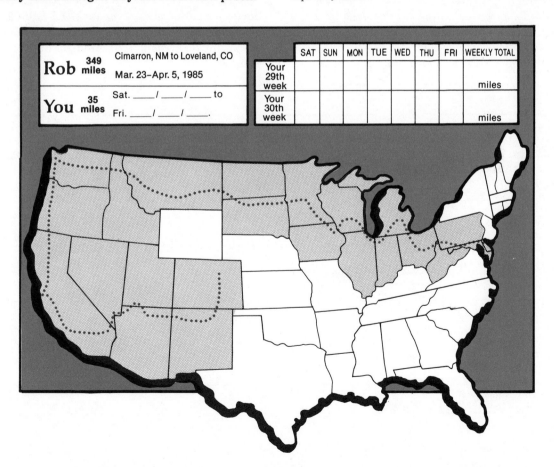

| | Cimarron, NM to Loveland, CO | | SAT | SUN | MON | TUE | WED | THU | FRI | WEEKLY TOTAL |
|---|---|---|---|---|---|---|---|---|---|---|
| **Rob** 349 miles | Mar. 23–Apr. 5, 1985 | Your 29th week | | | | | | | | miles |
| **You** 35 miles | Sat. ___/___/___ to Fri. ___/___/___. | Your 30th week | | | | | | | | miles |

# Foot Notes     Weeks 29 & 30

**29**   Handling the Rough Days _____

Early in the journey, I used to feel sorry for myself on those miserable mornings when I'd have to climb out of my motel bed, dress, pack, and step out into dark rain and puddles—30 miles of it perhaps. Watching motorists behind windshield wipers, I felt it wasn't fair for me to have to eat their rooster tails of spray spinning off their tires.

As the walk progressed, my attitude changed. I began liking those nasty days. Not that I prayed for them, but when they did come, I accepted them. "Rob, these are the days you'll remember," I'd say to myself in storms. I realized that the journey wouldn't mean anything if everything worked out perfectly. With that philosophy, you accept things as they are; you cope with discomfort in little chunks, trying not to worry about the full task of 30 miles ahead. "Rob, go out there for just an hour," I'd coach myself. "Just reach your next town; that's good enough for now. You can hang it up there for the day if you don't feel better." And so, mile after mile, town after town, I'd keep telling myself little white lies. And with some luck, I'd have 20 miles under my belt by early afternoon. Often by then the skies would be breaking blue.

**30**   Your Personal Foot Notes

_____

_____

_____

_____

_____

_____

_____

_____

_____

60

# Nebraska's Highway 30

Photo by Rich Fox, Grand Island Daily Independent.

**Tornado Time**  When you see the black funnel getting close, it's time to jump into a roadside ditch. That's the advice most Nebraskans gave me. This photograph was taken by Rich Fox of the Grand Island Daily Independent, right after 70 mph gusts busted up our news interview. The heart of the tornado struck David City, 60 miles east, that afternoon.

# Anyone for a Game of Highway Golf?

KIMBALL, NEB. — Robert J. Sweetgall found heaven yesterday in this sleepy little town with a single main street lined with "Mom and Pop" stores.

After walking 12 miles from Bushnell on the Wyoming border in 70-degree temperatures, he located a shady phone booth where he could air his feet on the concrete. From Bushnell, Sweetgall planned to walk about 10 hours until sunset and end up wherever that lands him on Highway 30.

Now heading east, Sweetgall left Colorado over the weekend, walked through a corner of Wyoming — the 26th state he's visited — and hit Nebraska yesterday. To date, Sweetgall has walked 6,565 miles. He aims to walk the length of Nebraska — 450 to 480 miles — in two weeks and a day.

As he enters the plains, Sweetgall said rising temperatures and tornadoes would be his biggest challenges. So far, he said, the winds have been good, but the temperatures are on the rise and that means potential foot trouble. He said his heels were still tender and he had a few bloody spots on his feet, "but they're still holding up."

In tests at the Medical Center Wednesday and Thursday, Sweetgall said the doctors found some improvement in his cardio-vascular system and some weight loss. The respite from his journey also provided him a chance to see his mother, who he said he hadn't visited with in a long while.

A dog named Budweiser gave Sweetgall some problems on Route I-25, just out of Fort Collins, not far from the Wyoming border. Its owners walked with Sweetgall to Wellington, Colo. where they helped him find a place to stay Saturday night in an old age home turned guest house.

Along the way he'd found a pancake house that served flapjacks the size of hub cabs. But that place didn't open until 8 a.m. and Sweetgall wanted to be on the road Easter Sunday a couple of hours earlier. He said the guest house owners gave him permission to help himself to breakfast, which meant he was on the road by 6:30 a.m.

Walking along fields of alfalfa, yucca plants and wildflowers, he watched ranchers go to church in their jeans and cowboy boots. Sweetgall said the landscape was "pretty barren. I didn't see anyone for nine straight hours on the way to Cheyenne (Wyoming)."

Along the way, Sweetgall carried a loaf of bread and bottle of soda to drink. On the outskirts of Cheyenne — "a kind of neat, old western town with old brick buildings, old hotels and cafes" — he found a truck stop that served free coffee. Sweetgall spent the night in Cheyenne and noted that he had now begun the eastern leg of his journey home.

Sweetgall's loose change collection is up to $74.92.

— AMY ZUCKERMAN

*April 11, 1985* —————————— *Week 31*

KEARNEY, Neb. — He doesn't really expect it to catch on, but "highway golf" is the way Robert J. Sweetgall wiles away his hours across the Great Plains.

"One day I found a golf ball beside the road and just tossed it ahead of me to see how far it would go. I watched it bounce down the road and ended up playing highway golf for about five miles. My best was 15 throws in a mile. My longest throw was about 150 yards, which I figure is equivalent to using a 7 iron," Sweetgall said.

"I also found a beautiful, brand new Spaulding Top Flight, but I sliced it into the rough by the side of the road and lost it," he said with a laugh. "A bad shot. I'll have to invest in a couple of golf balls to get through Nebraska."

Getting through Nebraska is proving a tedious task because of unseasonable heat and boredom, Sweetgall said.

And the dust being blown from the fields and the coal dust and cinders being blown off railroad cars, has been covering Sweetgall with dirt as he walks Old Highway 30.

"It's a dust bowl sometimes. And with the flat fields, there's nothing to stop the wind, no tree line. I hate getting sandblasted by the wind and eating dust, but I need it to cool off," he said.

"I've been drinking a lot of liquids — carrying 24-ounce bottles of soda or juice or water — but I'm eating less because of the heat."

Food has been inexpensive, he said: Pie a la mode for 90 cents; grilled cheese with tomato, 80 cents, a full, five-course meal, $3 or $4; a large lemondade, 35 cents with refills on the house. One restaurant displayed a sign that advertised coffee at "50 cents for the first hour and $2 all day."

He is walking in shorts, having taken a chance ("we could still get hail out here") and mailed home some of his heavier, winter clothing.

Sweetgall has walked 6,830 miles, 265 miles in the past seven days. He averaged about 36 miles a day for the past four days and is a day ahead of schedule. Nebraska, which he said will take 15 days to cross, is the third longest state on his walk route. He spent 31 days walking through California and 24 days walking through Montana.

"I thought when I left Cheyenne (Wyo.) that it would be a big deal to be heading east. But so far I've been battling heat and boredom and it hasn't been a big thing. There hasn't been a big change. When I start north from New Orleans, that's going to be the exciting part."

Wheat fields cover the western part of the state and corn fields cover the eastern part, he said. Sweetgall said the state is economically de-pressed, about 30 percent of the farmers have lost their farms to banks in the last two or three years.

"The state department of highways has posted signs that hay harvesting along the roads is prohibited because some farmers might clear shoulders of roads. Towns have shrunk. There's a lot of hardship. But a lot have survived, too," he said.

Asked by one student what he would do if he couldn't complete the walk, Sweetgall said he told the youth he never thinks about not finishing.

Sweetgall's roadside finds have included "a lot of car tools, a 1906 Indian head penny and my fifth wheat back (penny)." His loose change collection is $78.60.

*April 18, 1985* —————— *Week 32*

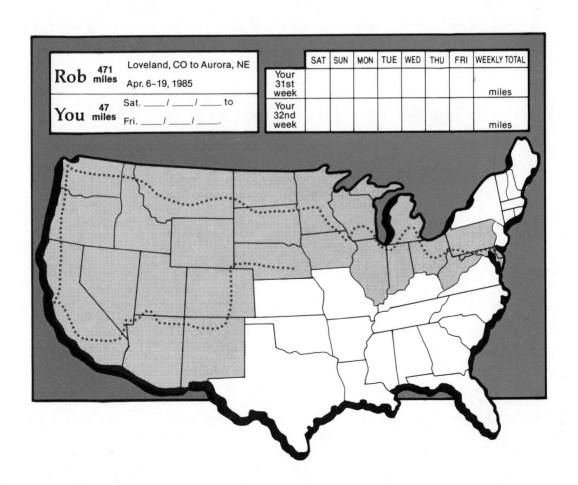

# Foot Notes  Weeks 31 & 32

## 31  Dealing with Dogs

*Everywhere I spoke, people wanted to know if I'd ever been bitten by a dog on my walk. When I answered "No," their faces showed disappointment—like "Oh, gee! We were really looking forward to a great bite story."*

*Sorry, folks. It just never happened. I've slept on couches with Pit Bull Terriers at my side, and I've walked up ranch drives guarded by Dobermans—but no bites. Here's why:*

*Whenever a dog moved toward me, I kept walking my normal course while sizing it up out of the corner of my eye. Two outcomes are possible: (1) the dog will go to its' territorial border and halt, or (2) it will keep coming. In a case (2) situation, I'll keep walking nonchalantly until the dog is within a few yards of me. Then I'll swirl around toward it in a Kung-fu motion, pointing my index finger at its head, staring it down. You've got to make eye contact. Sometimes I'll let go with a blood-curdling shriek. The whole act usually stops a dog dead on a dime. Of course it helps to be six foot two wearing thick winter mittens.*

## 32  Your Personal Foot Notes

# The Old Oregon Trail

**Roadside Maintenance** To prevent blisters, you take frequent "pit stops" like this one in St. Joseph, Missouri. The 6-step foot care routine is as follows: (1) strip feet naked, (2) swab feet clean, (3) air dry, (4) inspect carefully, (5) powder (try corn starch), and (6) lace up. Old tires make great roadside seats; so do cafe booths—except for the one in a St. Joseph restaurant where the owner threatened to call the police if I didn't vacate immediately.

Photo by Laura Embry.

# Show Me Missouri!

AUBURN, Neb. — Nebraska... still.

"Another day of country walking. It's been pretty much a lonely stretch: 450 miles of flat farmlands and then rolling farmlands. One blur of brown earth and cornfields," Robert J. Sweetgall said yesterday.

"It's more monotonous than anywhere else. You can't distinguish between towns. I pass through two or three a day. Mostly Federal brick architecture — a grocery, cafe, barbershop, tavern. Maybe a school."

Not a bad place, he said, just too much of the same thing, including unseasonably hot weather.

Sweetgall expects to enter Kansas (his 28th state) tomorrow, and Missouri (the 29th) the middle of next week at Kansas City. He has walked a total of 7,072 miles, 242 miles since last Wednesday. He said he has averaged 31 miles a day and is a half-day ahead of schedule.

He has been staying in motels, although last Wednesday he was invited to stay with Nick Ponticello and his wife in their trailer behind the gift shop of the Old Oregon Trail halfway point.

Ponticello bought the gift shop, which is shaped like a covered wagon, when the former owner thought the new interstate highway would kill business. The shop is located at the midpoint — 1,733 miles — between Boston and San Francisco.

Ponticello, 71, recently earned a degree in physical education from Kearney State College, which he has been attending off and on for 15 years, Sweetgall said. "He's thinking about going for his master's degree. Nick is an example of what Americans should strive for in older age. He exercises vigorously every day," he said.

"He runs 3-4 miles a day — fast — and has more energy than the averaage high school student."

It may be hot, but it is still only the start of spring. "The trees are blossoming with green leaves. Some fields are plowed brown and black earth. It gets dark about 7:30 at night. The humidity is climbing. The land is starting to roll more now that I'm approaching the bluffs of the Mississippi River. I'm coming gradually downhill, and I'm probably under 2,000 feet elevation," he said.

Sweetgall said the monotony of the walk through this part of the country has been broken only by the crash of storms, mostly heat and storm lightning at night. In a matter of minutes last Wednesday the weather went from clear blue skies to white clouds to black clouds and lightning bolts striking through the air. Three tornados struck within 50 miles of him, he said.

While in Grand Island last Friday he felt the winds of a tornado that struck David City, about 15 miles away. "I was sitting inside on the floor of a convenience store being interviewed for a newspaper story. The wind was blowing the pages of the reporter's notebook," he said.

On Tuesday he saw his first buffalo, when he passed three grazing in a pasture beside the highway.

*April 25, 1985* ——————————— *Week 33*

OLATHE, Kansas — During the past week Robert Sweetgall has walked east, south, west and south again as he has wended his way through Nebraska, Missouri and Kansas, his 29th state.

Sweetgall spent his last few miles in Nebraska pursuing his favorite new sport, highway golf, with Rotarian John Crotty. Crotty had last Thursday off and had planned to go golfing, Sweetgall said in a telephone call yesterday, "so I talked him into playing a hole on the highway."

Throwing the golfballs ahead of them as they walked, Sweetgall and Crotty walked about a mile and a half before Crotty decided he preferred golf course golf. He did leave two orange golf balls, one of which Sweetgall still has.

Thursday morning after leaving Crotty, Sweetgall walked to Brownville, the first Nebraska settlement on the Missouri River. After eating breakfast at an old hotel, he stopped at the post office, where he began talking with postmistress Melva Sage, a third genration member of the family that settled the town. She told him the town was a booming stage coach stop on the road west when a railroad bond issue failed in the late 1800s "and the town died."

After looking at a map and seeing that Missouri was just across the river, Sweetgall decided to alter his schedule and cross in to Missouri there. He said, "I was so close it seemed to be a good time to do it."

On Friday, Sweetgall walked a dirt road that was an extension of old highway 59. He said that after walking by little towns along a creek named Nodaway and Amazonia the prospects of finding a motel for Friday night were not good. When he came across a man in camouflage clothing who was hunting wild turkeys he asked for help and was directed to Ken Farris.

Farris told Sweetgall he was a former restauranteur who, after having a vision 17 years ago, became a prophet. "He was a very intelligent man who said the world is not destined for destruction. He thinks we're past the hard part," Sweetgall said.

Sweetgall reached St. Joseph, a city of 70,000, on Saturday. He called it a city in conflict, with the historical society fighting the demolition of sections of the old city while a mall is being built on the outskirts of the city.

On the south side of the city Sweetgall found one of the trip's best salad bars. Canteloupe, watermelon, honey dew melon, strawberries, bananas, blackberries, cheddar cheese, mush-

rooms, potato salad, cole slaw, chick peas, broccoli, 10 other fresh vegetables and a big plate and "all for 92 cents."

Saturday night in the little farm town of Rushville (population 40) he stopped at a bar for dinner. At midnight he walked into Atchinson, the first town in Kansas after crossing from Missouri. "It was prom night and the kids were raising hell," he said. He didn't get into a motel room until 1:30 a.m., 44 miles after starting the day.

On Sunday, Sweetgall was harassed by three young men in a car. Twice they sped close to him and on a third pass, threw a soda bottle at him. It missed. He notified police, "but I didn't see them again."

Sweetgall walked 238 miles in the past week. His loose change collection is $84.15.

*May 2, 1985 ———————————— Week 34*

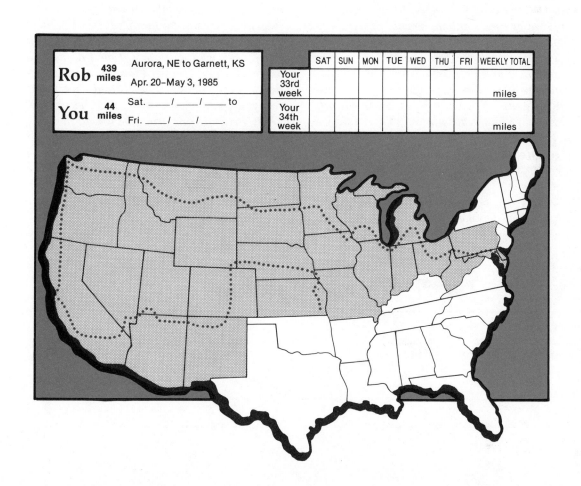

| | SAT | SUN | MON | TUE | WED | THU | FRI | WEEKLY TOTAL |
|---|---|---|---|---|---|---|---|---|
| Your 33rd week | | | | | | | | miles |
| Your 34th week | | | | | | | | miles |

Rob **439 miles**  Aurora, NE to Garnett, KS  Apr. 20–May 3, 1985

You **44 miles**  Sat. ___/___/___ to  Fri. ___/___/___.

33    **Walking on the Job**

*Rushville, Missouri. On old Highway 59, a neon-lit country tavern was my only chance for dinner. I was starved and entered.*

*Inside, four men in cowboy hats were picking away at electric guitars as men in coveralls and ladies in jeans stomped to blasts of "Devil with the Blue Dress On." I walked down a line of bar stools, claimed the last empty seat, and took a few odd stares. "Help yourself to the buffet," yelled the bartender in an orange net football jersey. "It's on the house."*

*I came back with two scoops of mayonnaised peas and runny slaw on a paper plate. The speaker vibrations were leveling my hill of peas. When the band broke, a tall blonde in a blue-jeans jumpsuit left her dance partner (he reminded me of the Camel cigarette man) and came up to me. "Nice legs," she said smiling. "Where'd you get that tan?"*

*"Oh, I'm just out walking the country. I get a lot of sun." I looked over to Camel Man. He was focused right on us. My eyes returned to my peas.*

*"Walking the country?" she laughed. "What for?"*

*"For health. So someone like you might see me and say, 'Hey, look what walking does for your legs. Maybe I'll walk too.' "*

*"I do enough walking at work," she said. "I'm in construction. We're working on a bridge job now. I walk up and down alongside those beams a hundred times a day. That's what you oughta do. You oughta quit this foolish walk of yours. It ain't doing you no good. What you need is a job in construction. Steel work." She raised her arms straight up to make sure I saw her figure. Then dropping one arm, she teased her long sandy hair around her ear, feathering her lips. "Listen here," she continued, "you don't have to walk across the country to get in shape. Just start working in construction. Look what it's done for me."*

*She had a point.*

---

34    **Your Personal Foot Notes**

---

# Pumps and Pipelines

**The Bank Walk**  On my return visits to Worcester, MA, I'd rush to my bank safe deposit box to squirrel away bunches of recorded microcassette tapes. This made room in my fanny pack for a few dozen blank tapes. The bulging footprints popping out of my chest are the replacement soles for my 5000 mile old shoes.

Photo by the Worcester Telegram & Gazette.

# A Woman Joins the Walk

TULSA, Okla. — Nowata, Watova, Talala, Oologah.

"The towns here are all named after Indians, and they're hard names to pronounce," Robert J. Sweetgall said.

"Oolagah was Will Rogers' birthplace, but he declared his birthplace as Claremore because he said no one but an Indian could pronounce Oologah."

The 18-mile walk from Nowata to Oolagah along Route 169 south "was easier done than said," Sweetgall joked in a telephone call yesterday from a school in Oologah.

Sweetgall entered Oklahoma, his 30th state, on Tuesday. He has traveled a total of 7,510 miles, 200 in the past week. He has averaged about 31 miles daily, more than a marathon a day.

This morning he was scheduled to walk into St. Francis Hospital about 10 a.m. for blood tests. He would later fly to the University of Massachusetts Medical Center in Worcester, Mass., arriving late tonight for testing tomorrow.

A week ago Sweetgall walked south from Kansas City, Kansas. "It was a 20-mile strip of houses south of Kansas City as you walk toward Center City. The farm land there is going fast."

He gave an unscheduled talk to students in grades 4-12 at Springhill. "Doug Allen, a high school junior who writes for the school newspaper, walked about three miles with me after the talk. I asked him at what level he thought students' attitudes toward fitness changed.

Sweetgall said the youth told him students start developing unhealthy habits at about age 12. "He said that's when the sixth graders start getting peer pressure from seventh and eighth graders, start to develop problems," Sweetgall said. "He was very perceptive."

A retired teacher in a salad bar ("I find one good salad bar every two days.") in Iola told Sweetgall that this part of the country experienced a growth spurt in the early and mid-1970s when high oil prices set speculators searching for oil and natural gas here. "But oil prices are down and things are shrinking back," Sweetgall said.

The land here is gently rolling farmland, he said. The main crops in Kansas are wheat, milo (a soft grain) and soybean. Oklahoma raises corn and horses.

"I see turned fields, nice black soil in certain areas. Green grass. The bluffs are fading out and there are more trees than in Nebraska. The land is more picturesque. The roads are narrow and winding, with little or no shoulder.

In Coffeyville Tuesday, six newspaper carriers rode up to him and asked him to autograph copies of the Coffeyville newspaper that contained a story on Sweetgall. "I told one I would autograph his paper if he promised he would deliver his papers one day on foot instead of his moped. He agreed."

As he heads south toward Texas, the earth "is turning red, the land getting a little more flat," Sweetgall said. "It feels like I'm going downhill. The humidity is up considerably over last week, and this is the highest heat stress since that 93-degree day in Nebraska a couple weeks ago. It feels like Louisiana, like Louisiana in the summer.

Sweetgall said his collection of loose change found on the roads now totals $86.21.

*May 9, 1985 ——————————— Week 35*

SALLISAW, Okla. — A electronics technician looking for a good way to stop smoking has joined Robert Sweetgall for a few days of walking.

Cindy White, a 32-year-old electronics technician for Williams Pipeline Co., saw Sweetgall on a television interview in Kansas City and decided to use her vacation for a walk, Sweetgall said.

"She has no walking experience except one walkathon. But she has to climb 300-foot water towers in her job, so she doesn't exactly lead a sedentary life," Sweetgall said. He said Ms. White, a former surgical nurse, plans to walk three days, which Sweetgall estimated would be about 90 miles.

She began walking Tuesday and had two small blisters by last night. Sweetgall said her shoes had to be sliced open on the sides to allow air to cool her feet. "She's going to have to walk my pace, though, which is about 3.5 miles an hour. Her goal is to walk at least the three days. She's going to give it her best shot," Sweetgall said.

Sweetgall returned to the University of Massachusetts Medical Center Friday for testing, which he undergoes every six or seven weeks.

"Everything is fine," he said. "No alarms, no breakdowns, no negative effects, no injuries."

He said he has lost about eight pounds, about one pound for every 1,000 miles he has walked. He weighs about 167 pounds, but he consumes 4,000 to 5,000 calories each day to try to maintain his weight.

Sweetgall spent Saturday with his mother, who had flown to Boston from Brooklyn, N.Y., where Sweetgall grew up. He returned to Tulsa Sunday.

A film crew from the "Ripley's Believe It Or Not" television program spent Sunday and Monday filming Sweetgall, which caused him to only make about 30 miles on those two days.

Monday night Sweetgall walked into Biggs Shoe Repair and Tire Co. to have his shoes resoled. He has walked 5,100 miles in those shoes which now have been resoled six times.

"Darl Biggs, who owns the combined gas station, shoe repair and tire company, said he has oil wells on his ranch but that he doesn't need a lot to get by," Sweetgall said. "He told me, 'I only tap the wells when I've got to get something for the kids'," Sweetgall said with a laugh.

"This is the 'Bible Belt.' At the bottom of a plastic menu on the wall of one little restaurant it read 'Jesus the Lord is Coming'," Sweegall said.

"The old farm towns are main streets with red brick that is covered with asphalt that has cracked and old brick buildings. In Haskell, you can still see the cast iron rings they used to tie the horses to on the curbs. The old highways go through the towns, some towns about half a mile off those old roads.

"From the road you can see the towns' water towers — pale colors, pastels, blues and silvers — no grain elevators here."

To date, his loose change collection, (money he has found on the roads) totals $89.03. He said he spends or gives the money away.

*May 16, 1985* ——————————— *Week 36*

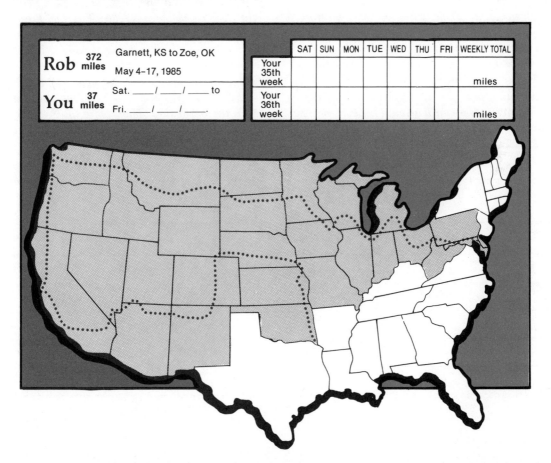

## 35   Forecasting War

*New Roads, Arkansas. Right off Highway 41, a man with bulging bug eyes lent me his shaded lawn for a foot break. On leaving I asked him, "Do you hear that humming in the trees? What is that?"*

*"Thirteen year Cicada," he responded.*

*"Is that a bug? Do they destroy things?"*

*"No. Not like a locust does."*

*"Why are they called thirteen year Cicada?"*

*"Because of their thirteen-year molting process. Some are of a seventeen-year variety, too. Before they die, they lay their eggs into a hole they bore into these pines trees. Thirteen years from now, those eggs will hatch out and make new ones. So you won't see this again here until around the turn of the century. But the important thing about the* Cicada *is that if you look on their wings, you'll see a* **W** *or an* **N**. *It'll have a* **W** *on one wing—always. And then on the other, it'll have either another* **W** *or an* **N**. *Now if they have* **WW**, *we're gonna have another World War. If they have an* **NW**, *it means 'No War.' "*

*"Come on, you're kidding."*

*"No. It's a real thing. A folk tale. My grandmother told me this, and she's been right ever since before 1900. The DeQueen newspaper did a whole research story on it. No one knows if it's genetics or what. But it never fails."*

*"Have you checked out this year's wings?"*

*"Sure have. My boy and I caught about a dozen the other day. They were all* **NW**. *Of course, I figured that meant Nuclear War."*

## 36   Your Personal Foot Notes

# Louisiana's Bayous

Photo by Robert Sweetgall.

**A Tribute to Louisiana** In Louisiana it was hard to walk into a grocery or cafe without someone opening up in friendly conversation. Several cafe owners came out on the shoulder of the road to offer me dinner. Near Alexander City, I stopped to say "hi" to a man selling watermelons. Next thing I knew we had spent an hour in Cajun conversation, carving up one of his 20-pound melons. Wayne Roy (24), taking it easy.

73

# Blisters in the Bayous

FOUKE, Ark. — The landscape resembles the Green Mountains of Vermont, but the weather is a typical, southern spring — hot, humid, and thundering.

"The miles are coming tougher," Robert J. Sweetgall said in a telephone call yesterday. "I'm pushing into heat and humidity, rain and thunderstorms. I'm fine physically, but I'm tired."

In the past week, Sweetgall has walked about 250 miles for a total of 7,895 miles. He has followed old Highway 59 out of Oklahoma to Highway 71 south down the Arkansas border to Texas and, now, back into Arkansas. He will spend about 10 days walking through Louisiana.

Sweetgall said Cindy White of Kansas City, a 32-year-old electronics technician for Williams Pipeline Co., walked with him for three days last week, including 35 miles last Wednesday. She walked a total of 80 miles. Despite a couple blisters and mild tendinitis, "she finished in good shape and could have walked more."

He said he has been walking through the Quachita National Forest. "The narrow, two-lane roads wind through pine, oak and maple trees. The asphalt is not very good, which makes it hard on the ankles."

On Friday, he made an unscheduled stop at a school in Hodgen, Okla., a town of about 1,000, as he was passing through town. "I spoke to about 120 students under a shade tree on the edge of the baseball diamond. There were only three days left of school, but the children seemed very interested. School starts early and gets out early because the children help on the ranches."

In Mena, Ark., Saturday night, "I got a haircut and learned the history of the town at the same time. The town, which has about 5,000 people, is one of the old railroad sites on the Pittsburg to Port Arthur line. The Main Street looks like many main streets in this area — old red brick buildings, two stories. Lots of boarded up and empty windows. In one town, Foreman, Texas, it looked like every one of ten brick buildings had been the grocery at one time. The faded word 'grocery' was painted on the top of each building.

"On the back roads here there are a lot of roadside places selling antiques, a lot of used cars, used parts, but still junk. Junk is big down here.

"Horses, cattle and chickens are big here ... hay, soybeans. I'm getting into a little cotton country and rice paddies. There are a lot of trees and mosquitoes. And the road is just full of squashed armadillos and turtles. Restaurants have fresh, cooked catfish, buffalo and frogs legs."

Sweetgall's loose change collection stands at $90.20. He found three cents in Texas.

*May 24, 1985* ———————————— *Week 37*

MARKSVILLE, La. — When a city swimming pool in Alexandria did not meet health standards, the mayor closed the pool and stocked it with catfish.

A woman talking with Robert J. Sweetgall in a small town outside of Shreveport thought he might be interested in talking to her 70-year-old neighbor, a man who had never worn socks.

Lost late at night on Route 71, Sweetgall knocked on a cabin door for directions and was greeted by a woman in a nightgown, a revolver strapped to her waist. "She was very pleasant," he said.

"There are a lot of good people here and more crazy people than in any other state," Sweetgall said with a laugh during a telephone call yesterday. "But they're the friendliest people around."

Louisiana is giving Sweetgall more excitement than he has had in many miles — a rousing reception in Shreveport, a scary late night walk through the swamps, high heat and blistered feet, poisonous snakes and an uncomfortable look at racial prejudice.

Sweetgall has his 16th and 17th blisters of the trip, similar to the painful blisters he got early in the walk last September.

The blisters are caused by temperatures in the high 80s and 90s, which heat the asphalt. The sides of his shoes are slit to let heat out and air in. (He is wearing his third pair, which have 5,600 miles on them and which have been resoled seven times.)

Sweetgall said that although the people through the northeast corner of Texas, Arkansas and Louisiana have been among the friendliest of the trip, he has been uncomfortable with the racial prejudice he has seen among some of the people during the past two weeks.

In Fouke, Ark., last Wednesday, a baptist minister stepped on his bathroom scale, saw he weighed 226 pounds and went out to mark off a one-mile walking course so he could start an exercise program. A few minutes later, Sweetgall knocked on the door looking for help in finding a place to stay. "He thought I must have been sent from heaven," Sweetgall laughed.

"There are oil pumps everywhere — church yards, the fronts of cafes, peoples' backyards, beside streams, in the middle of gardens. They look like they dropped from the sky and were set up wherever they fell," he said.

In Hosston Thursday night, Sweetgall stayed at the Black Bayou Motel. There was an oil pump outside the window of his $12.60 room. "It looked the way you would expect a $12 motel room to look — 1940s vintage and nothing matched," he said.

In Shreveport Saturday, Sweetgall said he was greeted by thousands of people wherever he walked.

A few hours later he was lost in the swamps. "That lift from the enthusiasm in Shreveport was gone. I was out there alone. It was really no man's land. One person was to have called ahead to friends who lived on an old plantation to put me up for the night," Sweetgall said. But when he got to the plantation, no one was home.

At 2:15 a.m., 47 miles into the day, Sweetgall saw a light on in a house and knocked on the door. A man answered and recognized Sweetgall from a newspaper story he had read. "He was a drapery salesman, and he let me sleep on a fitting table in the garage," he said.

On Tuesday, Sweetgall crossed the Red River, from the "Baptist side" of Louisiana to the predominately French-Catholic "Cajun country where I understand people are a little looser and live for cooking."

Sweetgall's "loose change" collection is at $93.60. The roads of Louisiana have yielded a toy Superman figure, a set of fish hooks, "the best pair of sunglasses I ever found (he has found six), wrenches (a popular roadside find), a red bandana and a dentist's bill, in addition to the many dead snakes, frogs turtles and armadillos.

*May 30, 1985* ——————— *Week 38*

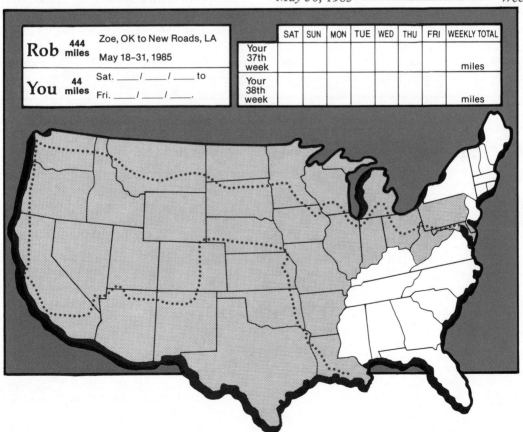

| Rob 444 miles | Zoe, OK to New Roads, LA May 18–31, 1985 | | SAT | SUN | MON | TUE | WED | THU | FRI | WEEKLY TOTAL |
|---|---|---|---|---|---|---|---|---|---|---|
| | | Your 37th week | | | | | | | | miles |
| You 44 miles | Sat. ___/___/___ to Fri. ___/___/___. | Your 38th week | | | | | | | | miles |

**Foot Notes**     **Weeks 37 & 38**

---

**37** Walking Straight ────────────────────────

You can read books on how to walk for exercise, or you can just walk. Trust yourself— you know how. Heavens, you've been at it long enough. No one has to tell you how to synchronize your arm and leg movements and breathing. That's the beauty of walking; you can be your natural self. Forget carrying all those heavy weights around your ankles and arms and on your chest. They distort your natural rhythm and biomechanics. Besides, they can damage your joints. God didn't intend for us to walk with 5-pound steel clunkers hanging off our limbs.

Just try to walk tall, trunk and head straight—without slouching. Your feet should rock from heel to toe with your arms swinging freely at your sides—and in the direction of travel. It helps to keep your feet close together pointing straight ahead. Sometimes in wet or snowy weather, I'll inspect my foot alignment by turning around to see my footprints. Both right and left prints should be nipping the edge of an imaginary white line.

This I was reminded of the night I slept in the Preston, Minnesota jailhouse. Above my mattress on the wall of the jail visitation cell block was a drunk driving poster. It showed a pair of feet tightroping along the white line. The caption read: "If you can't walk a straight line, we'll give you one month to practice."

---

**38**     👣 **Your Personal Foot Notes** 👣

_____

_____

_____

_____

_____

_____

_____

_____

# Cajun Country

**And Miles to go Before He Sleeps. . . .** Colfax, Louisiana. When Sheriff "Pop" Hataway got a dispatch call telling him there was "a crazy walker" out on the road needing a place to sleep, "Pop" said, "Bring him over. We can put him up." At midnight, "Pop" called Dru Richards, editor of the local weekly, who promptly climbed out of bed for the big news scoop. Dru's coverage later won a national journalism award. Also pictured is Grant Parish Jailer, Waylon "Lightning" Maxwell.

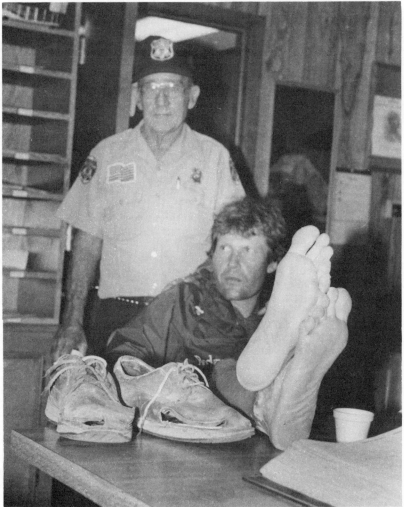

Photo by Dru Richards, The Colfax Chronicle.

# Living with Insects

NEW ORLEANS — This city of legendary seafood and rich, Cajun cooking may be a Nirvana to gourmets, but to a vegetarian athlete like Rob Sweetgall it's just another blood test along the way.

Sitting in a laboratory at the Ochsner Foundation Hospital — where he surrendered a few more cubic centimeters of blood for the scientists and chatted over the telephone to a newspaper reporter in Massachusetts — Sweetgall sounded rather wistful.

"The food is really good here," he said, "except I can't eat it..... I slept in the French Quarter last night at a little hotel called Maison Chartres and I asked for some recommendations for a good restaurant. They directed me to a place called, I think, "Petunias' but it was all seafood."

The southern cuisine is not without its special features even for vegetarians, however. Sweetgall said he has added a new item, grits, to his diet this week.

"They're not bad as long as you don't have too much of them," he said.

While he is walking during the day, Sweetgall said his diet "has gone almost totally liquid."

He said, "I can't eat anything solid during the day because I get really sleepy. The unexpected heat and humidity is exacerbating the situation even further, he said.

His perception of Louisiana food, weather and lifestyle intersected in several encounters this week.

"One day on the road I was getting in trouble with water. I couldn't find any. Then I came across this watermelon man. I got a 20-pound watermelon from him.

"We cut it in half and each of us sat down with a a carving knife, chatting about life in Cajun country. He was a Cajun. He had almost no formal education. He left the Corps of Enginneers and said "Hey, what's wrong with selling watermelons? He felt he had more control over his life with watermelons than anything else," Sweetgall said.

"He just takes life a day at a time, has a good time and doesn't worry about tomorrow. That seems to typify the Cajun attitude.

"While I was talking to him a car drove up and a man jumped out and said to me 'Are you Rob Sweetgall?' He had read about me in the Alexandria newspapers. He was Fred Roule, another Cajun, who was director of a youth leadership camp outside of Bunkie.

"At the age of 43 he had had a quadruple bypass operation and was now a strict follower of a low fat diet," he said.

"This man stands out to me as the person who's come closest to remove all the risk factors of heart disease from his life. He stopped smoking, adheres to a low fat diet, walks daily. He's also a marathoner. He told me that Louisiana has a very high incidence of heart disease and colon cancer. It's this whole attitude of high-fats food, live for today, exercise is secondary, smoke, drink etc.

Sweetgall said his days are nearly 16 hours long, since he tries to start walking at 5 a.m.

"I try to get an hour or two or three in before the sun gets high. That light factor increases by 20 or 30 percent my heat stress factor," he said. "That means a difference between going 60 to 70 minutes without a break or 80 or 90 minutes without a break."

The loose change collection in New Orleans has increased by about 75 cents a day — second only to the state of Michigan — bringing the total collection to $99.40.

FRANK E. MAGIERA

*June 6, 1985* ———————————— *Week 39*

BAY MINETTE, Ala. — "There are three ladies sitting here smoking cigarettes," Robert J. Sweetgall said early yesterday morning during a telephone call from Nita's Restaurant. "I don't think this walk is going to inspire them," to stop smoking.

"But that's all right. I'm aiming my message at 1 percent of the population. And I think it's been going pretty good."

Sweetgall has just begun his tenth month of walking, three-quarters of the way through his 50-state "walk for the health of it."

"I don't feel that much different physically than I did at the beginning. This walk is a job. I don't consider it to be any great personal challenge, any big ego trip. It's not some dramatic march against the elements to reach the finish line all tired and pooped out," he said.

"I don't feel I've changed that much from the beginning of the walk last September. I try to keep on an even keel, although the miles in the high heat and humidity here are the toughest," he said. "Now, 30 miles is like doing 40 in cold weather. It takes that much extra energy and time.

"But the South has surprised me a bit. The people are greater than I expected. A lot of support comes from the people in the communities; the kids walking up to me on the highway, the restaurant owners, the barbers and hairdressers, the police, the mechanic changing the tire who gives me the right directions or makes a phone call for me. That's been the thing that has really helped me on this walk; peoples' support along the highways."

Friday and Saturday he walked along the Mississippi Sound on the Gulf Coast. " Saturday I walked by beaches all day — wall-to-wall cars and people on blankets," he said.

Saturday night he stopped at a motel outside Gautier, Miss. "A two-and-a-half-inch roach climbed up my calf muscle and jumped off. I looked down on the carpet and all kinds of things were running around. I left," Sweetgall said. He walked until 2 a.m. when police at Pascagoula put him up at the city jail.

But he said bothersome insects are everywhere. "They're a big pain. There are black flies — they call them deer flies — that have been buzzing me and biting me. I feel like I'm walking with an electric razor around my head," he said with a laugh. "There are yellow flies that bite. There are fire ants that cover the ground and bite.

"It's all delta area, five rivers that run to the gulf and a big swampland. And fire ants all over. I took a break and sat on what looked like clean concrete for just a minute," he said. "Then I had to take my clothes off out on the highway to get the fire ants off me. My wrist and arms and backside are swollen from bites." He said he planned to seek medical attention because one arm was so swollen from the bite.

*June 13, 1985* ——————————— *Week 40*

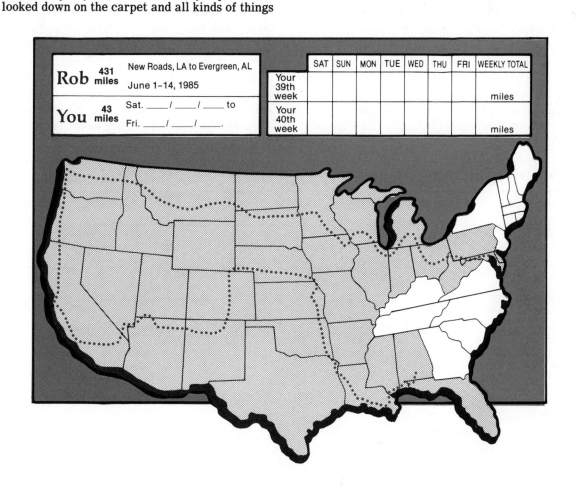

| Rob 431 miles | New Roads, LA to Evergreen, AL June 1–14, 1985 | | SAT | SUN | MON | TUE | WED | THU | FRI | WEEKLY TOTAL |
|---|---|---|---|---|---|---|---|---|---|---|
| You 43 miles | Sat. ___/___/___ to Fri. ___/___/___. | Your 39th week | | | | | | | | miles |
| | | Your 40th week | | | | | | | | miles |

## Foot Notes  Weeks 39 & 40

**39**  Highway Troopers

*The police had a habit of stopping me on my walks. Some asked for an I.D. Others just wanted to chat—kind of your basic highway coffee break with a strange-looking road animal. One Monday in Mesa, Arizona, on my first trek, it got more serious. I was detained 20 minutes in a police cruiser as the primary suspect in Sunday's Dairy Freeze robbery which was pulled off by a 6'2" blue eyed, blonde hair jogger whose description fit me to a tee. This I was told, after my driver's license cleared computer investigation.*

*In my home state of Delaware a trooper wrote me a citation warning for "walking in darkness without headlights" (a Delaware violation of the motor vehicle code).*

*Worst of all were the California Highway Patrol (CHP)—not all of them—just the few with heavy badges. California law states you can't walk the freeways if an "alternate"*

*pathway exists. What constitutes a realistic alternate route is a judgment call. To a CHP in a bad mood, a winding mountain road 20 miles out in the boondocks can qualify.*

*Contrary to their Hollywood image, Southern officers were the most helpful. In Bernadillo (NM), Cummins (GA), Colfax (LA) and Pascagoula (MS) they hosted me in jail. The morning after the night I slept in the Pascagoula holding cell, the warden woke me up at 7 A.M. and asked, "Would you mind giving a little talk at our Baptist Church breakfast meeting?" How could I refuse? During scrambled eggs, biscuits and grits, I spoke on my journey. As the meeting broke, I overheard one of the men say to the warden, "Hey, that guy wasn't a bad speaker. Where'd you get him?"*

*The warden replied, "Oh, we just pulled him out of jail this morning."*

---

**40**  Your Personal Foot Notes

80

# The Heart of Dixie

Photo by the Montgomery Advertiser.

**On the Map It Says . . .** The cool marble slab of Alabama's capital was one of the more ant-free spots to sit on for a map reading in the shade. In 1861, Jefferson Davis stood here addressing Confederate leaders. From these capital steps you can see much of Montgomery, Martin Luther King's church, and the boulevard he once walked on his march from Selma.

# Hills, Heat and Humidity

ROANOKE, Ala. — The walk now is heading north "and every step is bringing me closer to home," Robert J. Sweetgall said yesterday. "I'm not really happy about that because I know I'm not going to be happy when it all ends."

Sweetgall has walked 8,777 miles, 259 miles in the past seven days. He now has a little less than 3,000 miles remaining in his 12-month, 50 state journey.

"I'm making good mileage because of the rain, which has brought the temperature down, although it's real humid. Four of the last five days have seen drizzle, thunderstorms, all kinds of rain. But I'm a day-and-a-half ahead of schedule and averaging about 40 miles a day," he said.

Sweetgall said he required medical attentinon last week because of about 30 fire ant bites. He said, "My arm swelled to the size of a baseball bat. I got a shot and within a day I was feeling better."

Last Thursday he crossed the border into Florida then returned to Alabama. "I stopped at the town hall in Century, Florida. I was told that it was formerly called Teaspoon, but at the turn of the century they changed the name.

"There was a 14-year-old boy at the town hall who was putting in 56 hours of public service work for breaking into the school to steal computers. When I got there he was on his 56th hour. He had offered to spend the last hour sweeping the town hall floor by breakdancing in his T-shirt," Sweetgall said.

"There are a lot of oak and white pine trees; a lot of fields of soybean, cotton, corn and cattle. And there's kudzu everywhere. It's a leafy green Chinese plant they brought over here years ago for soil stabilization. It's worse than ivy and has just taken over. In some areas, it's all you can see."

Saturday and Sunday he walked the interstate. "The road's four lanes and pretty, but the prettiness wears off after about 10 miles," he said. "It's 50 to 60 miles of rolling hills. It gets old pretty fast."

At a convenience store in Fort Deposit on Sunday, a high school agriculture teacher suggested that Sweetgall take the more scenic road get back on Route 31 to go into Montgomery.

"As I came to the outskirts of Montgomery there were a lot of old, weathered shacks with porches and small gardens. Mostly black people who live on the outskirts of town. The children were very friendly and quick to wave. Then I turned a corner by a watertower and as I came into Montgomery I passed these mansions with the Greek corinthian columns, the manicured front lawns," Sweetgall said.

"I spent four hours in Montgomery, one of the few cities I've done sightseeing in. I toured the state archives. Montgomery's a real melting pot: people from all over the country live here."

"The big towns, those with over 5,000 people, generally seem to have a Wynn-Dixie grocery store, a Hardees or McDonald's, a Radio Shack, a weekly newspaper and a couple gas stations. Basically a lot of franchises."

Sweetgall is walking with his Goretex walking jacket over a wool jersey ("it's not warm because the wool breathes and it absorbs moisture") and a pair of running shorts.

He has put 6,500 miles on his third pair of shoes. He has had 17 blisters so far on the trip. "The asphalt here is not treating my feet too well," he said. "It's the popcorn-type asphalt with the little pointed stones. It's tough on feet."

Sweetgall is back on a country road, walking highways 22 to 34 to Atlanta, which he expected to reach tomorrow night.

His "loose change" collection is at $108.51.

*June 20, 1985* ——————— *Week 41*

GAINESVILLE, Ga. — "None of the ground is level out here," Robert J. Sweetgall said. "The hills have really picked up in the past week. I'm at the foothills of the Appalachias, the end of the Blue Ridge Mountains."

The hills have had an effect on Sweetgall, causing him to strain his left thigh muscle while walking down a steep hill outside of Alexander City, Ala., last week. "It was a long, steep walk and I just came down too fast," he said.

He said the strained muscle has bothered him occasionally in the past week, but, otherwise, he is in good physical shape.

"Most of the rain has stopped. We've had a dry, hot, humid spell," he said in a telephone call yesterday.

Sweetgall has walked a total of 8,970 miles, 193 miles in the past week. He said he expedted to cross into South Carolina this weekend, with Greenville. S.C., the next big town on his route.

Sweetgall crossed into Georgia about 2 p.m. last Thursday. "The owner of a package store just over the line in Georgia let me take a quick nap under his awning. He said most of the land around there used to be farm land. Now it's thick forest. There are a lot of fabric mills out here, too.

"The highway is mostly two-lane, lined with evergreens and oaks. The typical small towns are 5,000 to 10,000 people and the main streets have awnings supported by posts on the sidewalks and antique windows.

Friday Sweetgall reached Carrollton, "a city of 25,000-50,000 people that's about 50 miles outside of Atlanta. It's the start of the strip of development towards Atlanta: more quick stops, cafes, gas stations, more businesses. The towns are getting closer together. Interstate 20 has really opened up development to the west of Atlanta."

He said he called Jack Harvey, a salesman he had met on a flight returning from one of his periodic medical checkups at the University of Massachusetts Medical Center, who had offered to put him up.

"He was getting ready for a birthday party for his wife, Jackie, and had planned an open house for friends and neighbors. I told I would find some place to stay, but he came right out. He lives on the north side of Atlanta and drove 30 miles to pick me up," Sweetgall said.

"Developers want to develop that northern part of Atlanta and have offered homeowners in Jack's area $225,000 to $280,000 for their homes. They don't want the homes, just the land. "The whole area around Atlanta is built up. The road from Marietta to Roswell is pretty much new blacktop with a lot of real upper middle class yuppy homes: $120,000, three bedroom suburban homes, brick patios. Everything out there looks new. Just one little shopping center after the other with their computer, electronics and stereo stores."

The 'loose change" collection has reached $113.22.

*June 27, 1985* ———————————— *Week 42*

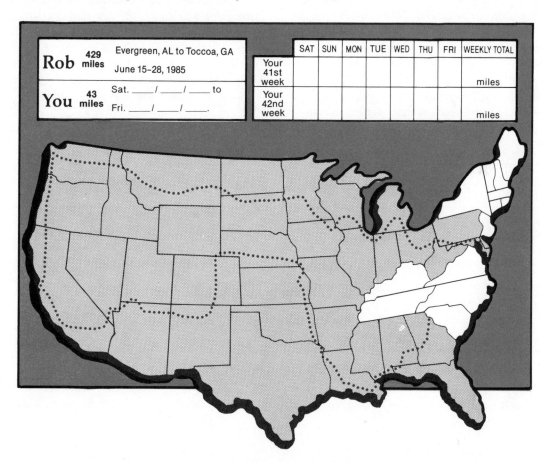

| | | | | | | | | |
|---|---|---|---|---|---|---|---|---|
| **Rob** 429 miles | Evergreen, AL to Toccoa, GA June 15–28, 1985 | | | | | | | |
| **You** 43 miles | Sat. ___/___/___ to Fri. ___/___/___. | | | | | | | |

| | SAT | SUN | MON | TUE | WED | THU | FRI | WEEKLY TOTAL |
|---|---|---|---|---|---|---|---|---|
| Your 41st week | | | | | | | | miles |
| Your 42nd week | | | | | | | | miles |

**41**    Your Basic Walker's Foot Care Kit ——————————————

*Wouldn't it be nice if you had a compact pouch that answered all your foot care needs? You could take it on hikes or on business trips and vacations, or just keep it handy at home.*

*Walking across America, I built such a kit using a supermarket plastic fruit bag as my pouch to hold the following: (1) rubbing alcohol (disinfecting and cleaning the skin), (2) iodine (disinfecting), (3) an insulin syringe (draining blisters), (4) matches (sterilizing the syringe), (5) bag of corn starch (powdering the feet), (6) Bag Balm (lubricating the feet in very cold weather), (7) lanolin (moisturizing the feet), (8) collapsible scissors (nail cutting and shoe trimming operations), (9) single-edged razor (cuttings), and*

*(10) moleskin (patching feet and shoes).*

*In a Biloxi (Mississippi) hardware store I bought a $1.99 wide roll of gray duct tape to patch up the flapping soles of my shoes. Beside that, the tape could be applied over reddened, inflamed skin as a bandage. Good-by moleskin. Best of all, it stuck beautifully to the bottom sides of my shoes—thus taking the brunt of abrasion while minimizing sole wear (I was very concerned about my soles lasting for the trek). About two foot-long strips of tape on my soles lasted nearly 30 miles, about a day of walking. And that's how I made it all the way north to Elkton, Maryland—2,200 miles—on just 1 set of soles—and six bucks worth of duct tape.*

**42**    Your Personal Foot Notes

# Great Smokey Mountains

Photo by The Atlanta Constitution.

**Covered in Kudzu** Over a century ago, when Southerners worried about soil erosion, a three-leaf Chinese plant named Kudzu (cŭd-zoo) was brought to and planted in the U.S. as an ornamental ground cover. The Kudzu grew like wildfire, spreading everywhere, smothering vegetation, climbing trees, and pulling down telephone wires. People have tried to uproot it, cut it, pull it, spray it—anything to kill it. But it won't quit.

# North by Northeast, Slicing Blue Ridges

MARS HILL, N.C. — The temperature has dropped a little as Robert J. Sweetgall walks uphill into the Appalachian Mountains, but it has brought no relief from a schedule that finds Sweetgall almost a full day behind schedule, with less than three months to go.

"I'll have to walk 235-240 miles per week now to keep on schedule," he said.

Sweetgall has walked 9,195 miles on his solo walk around America, 225 miles since last Wednesday.

"It will be tough making up miles because of the hills. Right now I'm walking a ridge between Blue Ridge Mountains and the Smokies. It's the lower Appalachian Range. I'm up about 2,000 feet in the air now, and the humidity is down a little bit. The weather starting to get a little cooler, with some nice misty rain, some good showers. It's helped."

"The roads out here are two types. One is a very narrow, very tight two-lane winding mountain road. It has steep falloffs on each side going into pine and oak forests. Very tight turns. All the roads are banked so the cars won't run off. That's murder on the ankles and affects the hips and calf and hamstring muscles. There is some foot pain but it keeps changing. The foot pain is like the old dresser drawer routine: you push one in and another one pops out," he said.

The second type of road is the four-land, divided highway. "Less scenic and more monotonous, although probably a little safer. But they're banked, too," he said.

This area of the country is a resort area, he said, with a lot of small, resort communities on lakes and rivers. "Lot of traffic and tourists."

Friday he walked through the small town of Alto, Ga. The mayor was at town hall dressed in his blue jeans. I asked him how the town got his name and he said they've been trying to answer that question since two out of state students first asked it five years ago. Nobody knows.

Saturday he crossed into South Carolina at Westminister. "Worse day on the whole tour for drivers. The drivers were terrible. I had more people coming at me ... some were inattentive. A lot of catcalls. Very illmannered."

He walked through Clemson, home of Clemson University, late Saturday. "Everything's orange, the school's color. All the driveways have orange tiger paws — at houses, shopping center's, restaurants I mean everywhere."

He stayed Sunday night at a motel where "everything — the floor, the furniture, the curtains — was orange."

The walk toward Greenville was another urban stroll, he said, with shopping malls of Winn-Dixies, Pizza Huts, hamburger stands, and furniture and fireworks stores lining the way.

Sweetgall's mother, Sylvia Sweetgall of Brooklyn, N.Y., and his aunt and some cousins met him on the highway as he came into Flat Rock. "They drove two-and-a-half hours from Charlotte. My aunt wanted to walk with me a ways, but the road was just too narrow and it was too dangerous. I spent the afternoon with them, but I just couldn't afford to spend the whole day."

Tuesday near Ashville he found a restaurant serving quiche, lentil soup and celery soda, "three things I don't usually get."

His loose change collection is at $116.20.

*July 5, 1985* ——————————— *Week 43*

TAZEWELL, Va. — Robert J. Sweetgall had more than his share of company this Fourth of July; a parade, marching bands and 25,000 people lining the streets of Kingsport, Tenn.

The Fourth was the highlight of a tough week for Sweetgall, who pushed in the heat and the rain through rugged, coal country terrain from Tennessee to Virginia, the very southern edge of Kentucky and back into Virginia again.

"I'm right on schedule, but it's tight," said Sweetgall, in a telephone call from a small town radio station. "I've been pushing really hard on schedule over the last week, averaging 38 miles a day for four straight days. We had showers 50 percent of the time, cooling me down and cooling my feet down."

Sweetgall said he was averaging 30 to 35 miles on the hot, dry days and 38 to 42 miles when it was rainy, doing most of his prime walking in the later afternoon and evening. "Typically," he said, "mornings highlight smokey, gray fog over the mountains that burns off mid- to late morning when the heat and humidity rises just when I'm getting sleepy and groggy."

Last Wednesday was Sweetgall's 300th day of the journey. As of yesterday — day 307 — he said he had averaged 30.8 miles per day and travelled 9,425 miles. He's in Hatfield and McCoy country — the Appalachians, river valleys and mountain gaps. Although he hasn't seen any, Sweetgall said there were bootleggers in the hills and marijuana — a big cash crop — growing in the fields lining the highway.

Last Wednesday he crossed the Tennessee state line along roads with switchbacks and hair pin turns and Baptist churches on every creek. A contact, Robin Miller, picked him up so he could march in the Kingsport, Tenn. Fourth of July parade the next day.

The highlight of the one-mile parade for Sweetgall was meeting two couples from Knoxville, Tenn. who drove up specially to walk with him. One child, Cary Bickford, 11, walked the whole route with him.

Back to his original spot that night, he walked all day Friday to Duffield, Va. along a "tough," 14-mile stretch without gas stations or groceries. Staying at the Ramada Inn that night, he said he was grateful to the owner for opening his restaurant for him and serving him a vegetarian meal.

Sweetgall made Big Stone Gap, Va. Saturday afternoon where the post master reopened the post office so he could buy stamps. It took several tries to get directions to Appalachia, the next town over, but Sweetgall walked the two miles on a "beautiful, winding, overlook road," on from there to a little town named Wise, the county seat.

Traveling winding roads on Sunday, Sweetgall made Elkhorn City, Va. that night. He walked in the heat along highways, dotted with little white churches, groceries and gas stations.

After a 5 a.m. breakfast, he pushed hard through Grundy, Va. On Monday, which he described as "more coal area."

His loose change collection was at $117.51.

AMY ZUCKERMAN

*July 11, 1985* ——————— *Week 44*

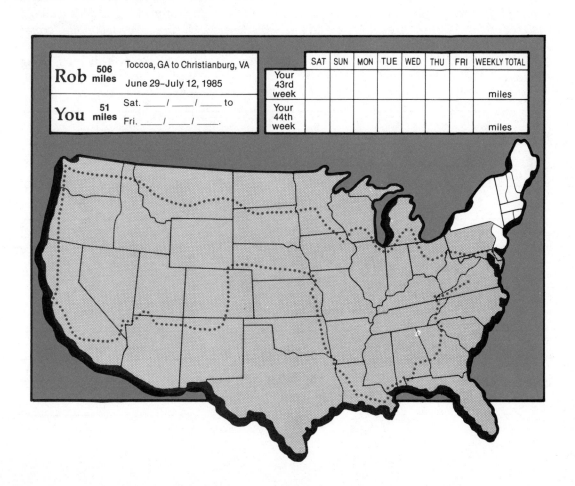

# Foot Notes     Weeks 43 & 44

**43** | Edward Payson Weston, Walker

Edward Payson Weston could walk 100 miles in a day—easily. Five hundred miles in six straight days was more of a challenge, but he did that too on numerous occasions. Not bad for a man born in 1839, a baby of 4 pounds, 4 ounces. Fully grown at 5'7", "Payse" as he was called, was still walking daily marathons at age 85. And if it hadn't been for a collision with a New York City taxicab in 1927 that dragged him for a costly, unmetered ride, Weston probably would have walked into the second century of his life. He died in 1929 at age 90.

In Weston's day, walking was king. Capacity crowds filled Madison Square Garden and Agricultural Hall in England to watch professional pedestrians compete in six-day foot races that made our modern-day triathlons look like 10K road races. That was 1880 Manhattan. Now we complain when we have to park in the remote lot.

But Weston did more than race. He walked across and around America, talking on street corners, in churches, and at town squares about the values of walking and his walking experiences. During one 3500-mile cross-country walk, Weston crawled for miles through a western blizzard on all fours, using a set of railroad tracks to guide himself through deep snow. Then he was 70.

**44** | Your Personal Foot Notes

# A Ridge & Valley
# Roller Coaster

**Edward Payson Weston** Back in 1909, when walking was losing ground to Henry Ford, the great 19th-century "ped," Edward Payson Weston set off from Santa Monica to promote walking. His goal—to reach New York (3611 miles away) in under 100 days. To the disbelief of skeptic news media (shown behind Payse) Weston completed the trek in 88 days, averaging 41 miles per day—at age 71.

# Homeward Bound

CHARLOTTESVILLE, Va. — "What Virginia has are the three Hs: hills, heat and humidity," Robert J Sweetgall said.

Despite those three Hs, Sweetgall has managed to average about 36 mile a day over the past 18 days to bring himself "dead even with schedule. I've been in Virginia since July 5, with one-day walks into Kentucky and West Virginia.

"Sunday it was 95 degrees with 90 percent humidity. I fell asleep walking up a hill and almost keeled over. I stopped and knocked on a door to buy a soda from a family and ended up taking a nap in the shade between some old, pinstriped velvet auditorium seats they had outside the house.

"I've been going into midday slumps, between 11 a.m. and 3 p.m. That is the toughest part of the day, physically, although the black asphalt is at its hottest about 6 p.m.," Sweetgall said in a telephone call yesterday from this city of about 45,000 people. "I miss the cold wind on the prairie."

The highway here is called The Roller Coaster and it follows a seemingly endless series of half-mile- to mile-long hills. "There's not a flat piece of earth out here. The road winds because of the way they had to cut into the mountains.

"Most of the past week I've been walking in the Appalachia's Ridge and Valley Range. Half the days have been rainy, and I've done better on those days," he said.

"I've been on highway 90 percent of the time this past week. It's a four-lane, divided highway with either a grass or forest median strip. About 70 percent of the time I walk against the traffic and about 25 percent of the time with the traffic to give my ankles a break on the banked turns."

Sweetgall said the pace of his journey seems to be getting faster. "Right now I'm just trying to stay on an even keel. I don't know what to expect in the next few weeks, although it's a real tight schedule. Things just seem to be moving too fast," he said.

He said that as he nears the Sept. 7 finish line in New York City the walk "kind of feels like the last day of school did — you wanted it to end but then you didn't.

Sweetgall said he doesn't expect the heat to end until the walk does. "In the morning the sun seems to hit suddenly. One minute it's 65 degrees with low sun and the next minute it's 85-90 degrees with a high sun. I've been carrying a red bandana," he said.

"I try to dip it in ice water to swab my face and neck. A lady yesterday in Shady's Cafe made a homemade ice tray from a Pepsi carton and a plastic bag for me to cool my feet on while I ate jello and fruit cocktail.

"In the last 36 hours I've walked with a cattle rancher-car dealer, the manager of a hospital lab, a retired DuPont Co. secretary, a 5-year old boy named Matt Falkner who walked the furthest, 3.3 miles, and news photographers, reporters, cameramen and a school teacher."

Sweetgall said he has been eating a lot of biscuits "and getting some good home meals with squash and eggplant and zuchini."

His loose change collection is at $120.10.

*July 18, 1985* ——————— *Week 45*

RISING SUN, Md. — Robert J. Sweetgall has been this way before.

Forty-six weeks ago he started his walk through all 50 states from nearby Newark, Delaware.

"It feels good. I feel like I'm getting back into my home territory. It's kind of exciting to return, to see the highway that you left 10 months ago and to reflect on all the time that has passed," he said yesterday.

He planned to go 20 miles out of his way yesterday to cross the Susquehanna River because he was uncertain whether he would be permitted to cross the Highway 40 bridge over the river. "I tried it once on bike and almost got the bike confiscated. The police made me take the bicycle back a mile to the toll bridge, pay the toll, then lectured me. I've come almost 10,000 miles and I don't want a hassle now," he said.

He returned to Worcester last Thursday for testing at the University of Massachusetts Medical Center. He said he thought he performed poorly on the tests because of the stress of walking 500 miles in the past two weeks to catch up to schedule and the effect of the heat and humidity.

However, he reported he has had a reduction in body fat since the walk started and has dropped 10 pounds to 163 pounds, despite eating 4,000 to 8,000 calories a day to maintain strength.

Sunday he walked through the Manassas battlefield in northeastern Virginia, "rolling pastures of hay where one of the major battles of the Civil War was fought. At the battlefield I drank as much water as I could because the next water was six miles away and it was a terribly hot day."

Monday he walked into Washington, D.C. "It was there that Sweetgall began his 10,600-mile walk-jog around the country in 1982. That trek began as a jog with a friend following in a van and ended as a walk alone when he found walking caused less injury and his friend left about halfway through the trip.

Sweetgall was interviewed by a reporter for The Washington post who last summer rode a bicycle from Washington to Los Angeles. "We had a lot in common. He had to lie to his mother, too, at times so she wouldn't worry," Sweetgall said.

"The last half week it has been getting to be more industrial highway; more tractor-trailer trucks, more concrete trucks, more steady rush hour traffic, dust, grit and rocks. It's getting to be the East, no question," he said with a laugh.

"Tuesday night I was on the inner harbor in Baltimore. They redid the whole downtown section of Baltimore, and it is one of the cleanest, prettiest downtowns I've seen on the tour. It's one of the prettiest walks I've taken. you could look up at the skyscrapers and watch blue sky turn fiery orange, reflected in the windows, the people dining out a open cafes, the frigate Constellation sitting at the harbor, the tourists charting their way on brick inset piers. . .

"However, later I asked a cop where to catch Route 1 downtown, and he said even the police don't like to go there. he said 'We've lost control of that area and you'd never make it through there at night.'"

His loose change collection is at **$122.32**.

*July 25, 1985 ————————— Week 46*

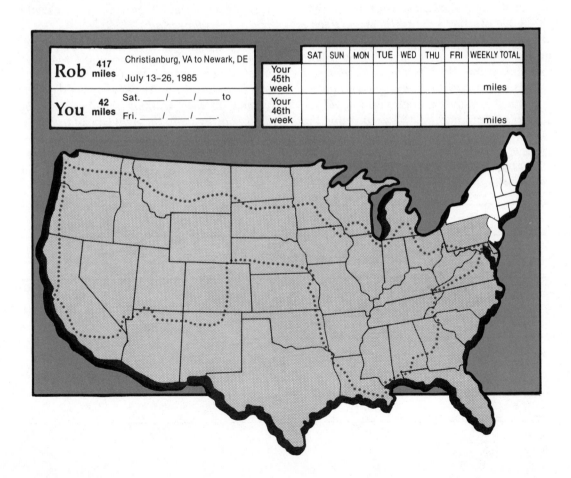

| | | SAT | SUN | MON | TUE | WED | THU | FRI | WEEKLY TOTAL |
|---|---|---|---|---|---|---|---|---|---|
| **Rob** 417 miles | Christianburg, VA to Newark, DE July 13–26, 1985 | | | | | | | | |
| Your 45th week | | | | | | | | | miles |
| **You** 42 miles | Sat. ___/___/___ to Fri. ___/___/___. | | | | | | | | |
| Your 46th week | | | | | | | | | miles |

**45** **Eat and Walk, or Walk and Eat**

In this age of "how-to wisdom" we listen to experts for solutions that our forefathers determined by common sense. "When to eat and when to walk" is a classic example. Everywhere I go, people ask me, "When should I walk?"

Frankly, I don't think it makes much difference—as long as you eat lightly—which isn't a bad idea anyway. On my journey, I was eating 8 to 10 times a day. Light meals—mostly 400 to 600 calorie feedings. I walked when I had energy. I ate when hungry. Basic animal instinct. Often in sub-freezing weather (Montana and central Washington in December), I rigged up my plastic feedbag of peanut butter and honey sandwiches such that I could extrude blobs into my mouth by squeezing the bag without removing my gloves. One squeeze every ½ hour was worth about 200 calories—3 miles of fuel—with no time lost. And never did such "walking meals" cause me cramps or indigestion. Keep in mind, though, I was: (1) eating light, (2) walking easy, and (3) eating non-greasy, non-fried, easily digestible foods.

Realize though: that "walking" and "digestion" are competitive processes. Both require increased blood circulation. Together they can be compatible but only if both are kept at a moderate level. So if you plan to do a hard walking workout, either walk first, or wait a few hours after eating.

Famished in Gainesville, (GA), I made the mistake of stuffing down double plates of mashed potatoes, black-eyed peas, and kidney beans on rice in the heat of the day, and wound up sleep-walking my way to Lula. Twice I drifted into the right lane of traffic before crashing for a nap on an office swivel chair that was for sale at a roadside antique shop. A Mexican-style siesta after lunch would have been wiser.

**46** 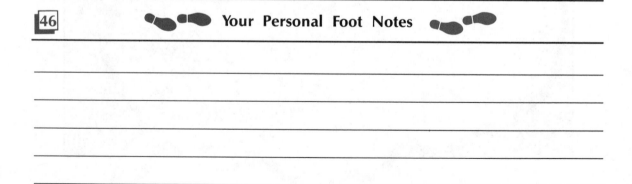 **Your Personal Foot Notes**

# The Hudson Valley

**Sitting on the Dock of the Supermarket**   Troy, NY. Many cold meals were eaten in the shade of supermarket loading docks. Here it's 2 pints of jello ala fruit cocktail while cutting new inserts for my walking shoes. Nearly 8000 miles old, these shoes still had to hold together for the final 700 miles. That didn't matter to the security guard who demanded my dock departure immediately.

Photo by Steve Lanava, The Evening Gazette.

93

# Surviving on Eastern Industrial Highways

BRUNSWICK, N.J. — Rob Sweetgall returned last week to where his walk across the country began 322 days and nearly 10,000 miles earlier.

He stayed just long enough to remind his friends that contrary to what they thought, his walk wasn't really over yet.

Upon his return to his hometown of Newark, Del., where the walk began late last summer, he was greeted by 30 employees of the Otts-Chapel plant of W.L. Gore Associates, the manufacturer of the breathable, waterproof fabric, Gore-Tex. They walked with Sweetgall for more than five miles back to the plant which is actually just over the state line in Elkton, Md., and retraced some of opening miles of Sweetgall's walk.

The company sponsored a reception for Sweetgall and he addressed about 100 employees. The clothing Sweetgall is wearing on the walk is made of Gore-Tex.

Sweetgall said he almost did not make it to Delaware on time. He found himself running about 15 miles behind schedule the evening before and decided to save himself 27 more miles along an alternate route by crossing the Pulaski Highway Bridge (Route 40) over the Susquehanna River. The bridge prohibits pedestrian traffic and, according to Sweetgall, has hardly enough space for a pedestrian to walk beside its four lanes of vehicular traffic.

"I waited for the first solid darkness at about 9:30. I put on my Gore-tex pants, so I was all dressed in dark blue. I downed a milk shake for energy and took off for bridge.

"I was hoping for just 40 minutes undisturbed by the police. I figured I could get across the bridge and then duck around the toll plaza into some high grass. About one-third of way across the bridge I got the feeling that some motorist was going to squeal on me.

"Sure enough right at the midspan a policeman stopped me."

Several other police arrived on the scene and although Sweetgall had explained about his journey and asserted that he wasn't about to interrupt 10,000 miles of continuous walking for a half- mile automobile ride, they were still adamant about allowing him to walk the bridge.

At this point Sweetgall said he was resigned to walk the alternate route rather than ride across the bridge.

"Then I said, okay look, tomorrow morning I've got an interview with The Associated Press. The whole country is going to read about the police who made me walk another 27 miles rather than let me go across that bridge.

"The officer in charge thought it over for a minute then ordered one of the others to get some release forms so I could sign off on any liability. I signed the forms on the hood of the police car at about 11:45. Then he told me to walk the middle of the white line at the side of bridge and not to deviate. He said don't try any smart stuff and when you get to the toll plaza don't talk to anybody, just keep walking."

FRANK E. MAGIERA

*Aug. 1, 1985* ———————————— *Week 47*

ALBANY, N.Y. — Robert J. Sweetgall turned east today from this upstate capitol city , heading toward New England and the final month of his cross-country walk.

Sometime tonight or more likely tomorrow he expects to cross the state line into Bennington, Vt. on Route 7.

During the past week Sweetgall has been walking north through New Jersey and New York along the Hudson River. He has walked a total of 10,320 miles but said the last hundred were some of the most unpleasant.

"Things have gotten a bit unfriendly in New Jersey and New York," he said in a telephone call from Catskill, N.Y., yesterday. "It's something like the New York don't-bother-me attitude. It's something that I've rarely seen in the country."

Sweetgall said the general unfriendliness came to a head earlier this week when he found himself in southern New York during a regional festival that glutted the hotels and motels with tourists. On several nights he was unable to find a motel with a vacancy. Motel desk clerks refused to allow him to sleep outside on their property or in basements as he has in other parts of the country. In some cases the desk clerks even refused Sweetgall permission to use the motel telephone to inquire about accomodations elsewhere.

Sweetgall said he found another $10 bill this week, his second in two weeks. That brought his loose change count to $157.25 and his green money finds up to $23.

The $10 find also was a fitting occasion for Sweeetgall to walk several miles with his old friend, ultra-marathoner Harry Berkowitz of Piscataway, N.J.

"Harry runs in every sort of race from a mile through the six-day, 300-mile races," Sweetgall said."Harry is the person who introduced me to loose change. In the last 20 years he's collected more than $700."

Sweetgall said he has been very tired this week and seems to be devoting more time to media interviews and caring for his feet.

"Together that takes about five hours a day," he said. "Sometimes I'm on the phone for four hours."

New Jersey was mostly industrial grit, dust, fumes and slums he said. "What I'm seeing now is a lot of little taverns, motels and diners. There are a lot of Italian restaurants and pizza parlors. I'm walking on the east side of the Catskills and the farther north I get the better it looks," Sweetgall said.

He got a kick earlier this week in Kingston, N.Y. when he stopped to browse in a shopping mall bookstore and came across his own recently published book on fitness walking.

"That was the first time I'd seen it. It kind of sent a little chill down my spine to see it out there. It's a little like seeing your first baby," he said.

Some members of his family walked with him near Westfield, N.J. including a young cousin and his elderly aunt who is approaching 80.

FRANK E. MAGIERA

*Aug. 8, 1985* ———————— *Week 48*

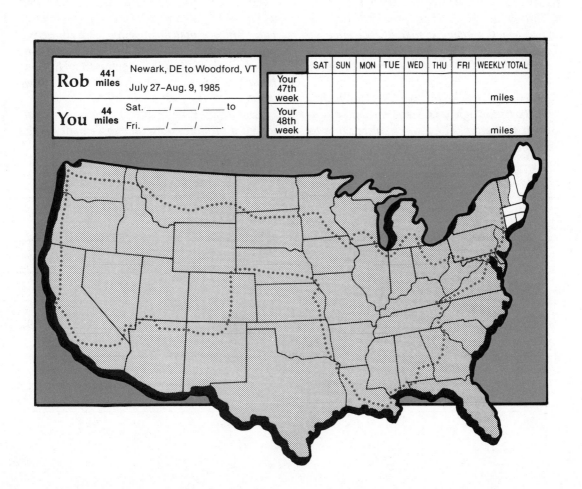

| | | SAT | SUN | MON | TUE | WED | THU | FRI | WEEKLY TOTAL |
|---|---|---|---|---|---|---|---|---|---|
| **Rob** 441 miles | Newark, DE to Woodford, VT July 27–Aug. 9, 1985 | | | | | | | | |
| | | | | | | | | | |
| **You** 44 miles | Sat. ___/___/___ to Fri. ___/___/___. | | | | | | | | |

Your 47th week — miles
Your 48th week — miles

# Foot Notes     Weeks 47 & 48

**47**   **Eating Off the Highway**

It wasn't easy eating off the highway—particularly in the desert and prairie regions. There, balancing the diet meant selecting the right proportions of peanut butter, jam, and whole wheat bread. In the Mojave Desert, I'd walk 30 miles up to an Interstate cafe to find my menu choices limited to white toast, eggs over, a premixed milkshake, soda, and candy. Fast food "carbos" with a little grill grease to slide it down. Across Montana, taverns served me the "veggie special"—a slice of American cheese microwaved on a hamburger bun. In Rock Creek, supper was three of those.

Whenever I walked into a "big" town that owned a traffic light and salad bar, I'd be sure to visit the latter. There my goal became to eat as many "colors" as possible. A great meal was an 8-color plate: **red** (tomatoes), **orange** (carrots), **yellow** (corn and chick peas), **green** (string beans, spinach, and broccoli), **white** (potatoes and cauliflower), **maroon** (kidney beans), **purple** (beets), and **beige** (mushrooms and black-eyed peas). The more colors, the greater the variety of vitamins and minerals. It really works out that way. That's what the analysis of my food logs indicated as I measured and recorded every single meal I ate (3 plastic measuring cups were clipped to my waistpack). Those logs, computer analyzed at the U. of Massachusetts Nutrient Data Bank System, showed no major nutrient deficiencies. Yes, I met my RDA's.

And just for the record, I never once swallowed a vitamin/mineral supplement on the entire walk.

**48**    Your Personal Foot Notes

# New England

Photo by Steve Lanava, The Evening Gazette.

**Bridge Crossing**   I love walking bridges. Each have their own character. Steel trusses, wood planks, vibrating walkways. In Seattle I raced across a drawbridge as the platforms started to crank open and rise. Misjudgment. Luckily I made the jump. Crossing illegally on the Route–40 Susquehanna Bridge (pedestrian prohibited), the Bridge Police read me the "riot act." But here in Hoosick (NY), it's just peaceful woods all around with Vermont ahead.

# Summer on the Rocky Coast

NORTH BERWICK, Maine — Robert J. Sweetgall's walk has not been lonely, as old friends and new acquaintances have popped up during the past week to spend time with the walker.

"I was at a phone booth in Bennington on Saturday when a girl in a black pickup truck waved out the window and said 'Hi, Rob.' She was Michelle LeBlanc, the daughter of the owners of the Peter Pan Motel, where I stayed during my perimeter tour of the country two years ago," Sweetgall said yesterday.

While walking to Wilmington on Sunday, Sweetgall was stopped by a magazine writer who had interviewed him for a story on walking. "She and her husband were on a weekend trip. I had never met her, but she said she recognized me from the photograph that ran with the story."

He also stopped to talk to a husband and wife from Holland who are bicycling through New York and New England. A little further down the road he met a former acquaintance from Boston who was driving by on his honeymoon.

"As I was climbing a hill out of Brattleboro about 7 Sunday morning, a mint green taxi cab stopped beside me. It was John and Cathy Hall of Grafton. He runs the taxi company and a garage in Grafton. They had been reading the Evening Gazette stories and made the two-hour ride up to Vermont. John, who severely damaged his knee in a motorcycle accident and recently had it re-broken and pinned, walked 11 miles with me."

Sweetgall said Mrs. Hall, who stopped smoking cigarettes two weeks ago, walked about two miles.

As he approached Keene, N.H., Sweetgall was joined by Kathleen Brow, a 67-year-old Winchendon resident who had been following his progress in the newspaper and decided to drive out and find him on the road. She walked about a third of a mile.

The walk through Vermont and south-western New Hampshire was disappointing, Sweetgall said. "It was tourist gift shops, cheese, moccasins, sheepskin rugs, maple syrup, and little wood nick trinkets. The roads are full of litter and cans, despite the Vermont nickel deposit."

It wasn't until he got to Dublin, N.H., on Sunday "that I felt like I was really in New England.

Up to that point most of the towns have been sort of a homogenized America.

As he left Peterborough on his way to Manchester, N.H., Monday, Mrs. Brow, her sister, Mary Campbell and Mrs. Campbell's daughter, Laurie Campbell, plus their niece and nephew, Corey and Ashley LaPointe, drove up.

"Mary and Laurie walked about three miles with me, then Corey joined us. He's 3. He walked six-tenths of a mile but by the end of the road we were pulling him out of the forest because he kept veering off into the woods," Sweetgall said and laughed.

His loose change collection is at $161.98. He found $2.26, mostly quarters on Vermont roads.

*Aug. 15, 1985* ———————— *Week 49*

BOSTON — It was late and the motels along the Maine coast were filled. But Robert Sweetgall needed a place to stay so he welcomed the offer to sleep in the back of a Toyota hatchback that was at a garage for repairs.

"I slept well, but I think the car I slept in the night before was roomier," he said in telephone call yesterday.

Although Sweetgall is approaching the Sept. 5 end of his 11,700-mile walk of America with people honking on the highways and newspaper and radio interviews appearing daily, he still often finds himself with no place to stay at the end of the day.

"It was tough in Maine and New Hampshire because this is the tourist season. There's really no place to stay."

Sweetgall crossed into Maine last Wednesday. "Fresh air. The smell of hay, cows, and corn stalks. I enjoyed it. It was open country until I got to Route 1 and Kennebunk. Then it became industrial, commercial.

Friday he walked into Portland and got his first look of the trip at the Atlantic Ocean from a bluff overlooking Casco Bay.

"Downtown Portland's a great place. Craft shops, gourmet food shops, touristy gift shops ... I liked it. A lady selling bagels said it's the closest thing to Greenwich Village."

He headed south and by midnight Friday had called motels and police and fire departments looking for a place to stay. "I finally stopped at a place that makes video film. The man on the third shift said I couldn't sleep inside because of security reasons, but he let me sleep in the back of his Pacer. He woke me up when his shift ended at 4 a.m. and I started walking again."

He walked south towards Rye Harbor, N.H., but by nightfall, for the second straight night, had not found a place to sleep. "The attendant said I could sleep in the back of the Toyota, which was there for engine repairs.

"Sleeping in the cars wasn't bad, but I miss the hot water and showers," Sweetgall said.

On Sunday he switched to Route 1A, and walked by the cottages and homes along the Atlantic Ocean, then past the beaches at Rye and Hampton, N.H., and Salisbury, Mass.

"I felt awkward walking along the boardwalks with all the bathing suits and bikinis, people with hardly anything on and me in my full walking gear. I felt overdressed."

As of last night, Sweetgall had walked 10,762 miles, 210 miles in the past week. He planned to walk to Plymouth today. Tomorrow he will walk from Plymouth to Wareham and the Buzzards Bay region.

At 5 p.m., Aug. 29, Sweetgall will walk from City Hall down Main Street, across Thomas Street to Commercial Street and back to City Hall. He has invited all Worcester County residents to join him in that one mile "walk for health."

His loose change collection for the walk is now $166.25.

*Aug. 22, 1985* ———————— *Week 50*

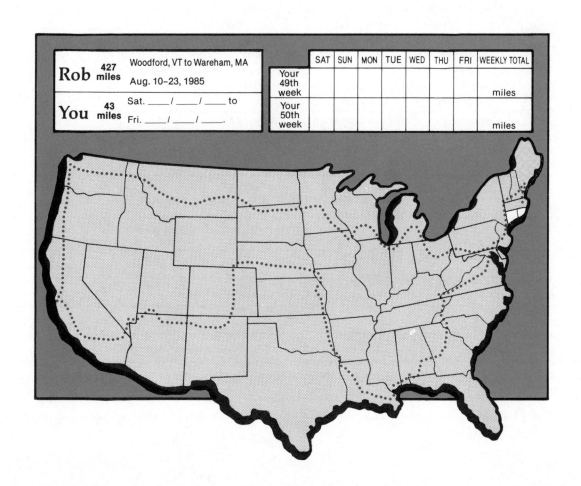

| | | SAT | SUN | MON | TUE | WED | THU | FRI | WEEKLY TOTAL |
|---|---|---|---|---|---|---|---|---|---|
| Rob 427 miles | Woodford, VT to Wareham, MA Aug. 10–23, 1985 | | | | | | | | |
| You 43 miles | Sat. ___/___/___ to Fri. ___/___/___. | | | | | | | | |
| Your 49th week | | | | | | | | | miles |
| Your 50th week | | | | | | | | | miles |

**49** Creative Sleeping

*Ever get caught in a strange town, wondering where you'd sleep that night? I did. A few hundred times last year alone. Below is how things turned out.*

### Sleeping Around America for a Year

181 Motels (4 walls & sanitized cups)
78 Homes of strangers (trust)
36 Homes of old friends
16 Hospital beds (sickening)
10 Trailers/motorhomes
7 Jails (prisoner's breakfast)
7 Guest houses (still a few left)
5 Churches (leave a donation)
3 Cars & hatchbacks (no shower)
3 Tavern & cafe lofts
3 Casinos (straight to bed)
2 Airplanes (red-eye specials)

2 College dorms
2 Hotel lobbies (no vacancy)
1 Fire station (by the pool table)
1 Old age home (quiet evening)
1 Drapery shop (on the fitting table)
1 Motel towel room
1 Grocery attic
1 Church closet (a little tight)
1 Newsroom (small town paper)
1 Grain elevator (in harvest season)
1 All night walk
0 My own bed

*364 Nights on the Road*

**50**  **Your Personal Foot Notes**

# The Big Apple

**Bronx-Busters** Three locals stopped to check out the "weird dude" who was tending his feet beneath a condemned apartment overlooking New York's sidewalk trash. When they saw my shoes, they believed my story.

Photo by John Lusk.

Photo by Steve Lanava, The Evening Gazette.

**The Last Mile** On the Brooklyn Bridge, I felt the journey slipping away. It was the saddest mile of the walk. You can't prepare yourself for the shock of it all: The End. And yet everyone there expected me to finish happily. The balloons, banners, and bands were inappropriate for this seat-of-the-pants mission. For me it was the end of the best year of my life. So I just cried.

# The Road Show Ends

WORCESTER — "I know there's a week to go, but for me Worcester is the climax of the walk," Robert J. Sweetgall said yesterday. "The people who have been following the walk in The Evening Gazette, those who've written during the year . . . there's been a lot of support and I feel really good about being here.

"And if you added up all the miles I've walked on the treadmill for medical tests at the UMass Medical Center, I've walked more miles in Worcester than in any city in the country," he said. "I've also spent more time here than anywhere else in the past year."

Sweetgall has returned to Worcester periodically during the past year for testing to study the effects of walking on the human body. A native of Brooklyn, N.Y. who lives now in Newark, Del., Sweetgall said Worcester has been his "home port" during the past year.

Worcester marked Sweetgall's 11,000th mile on the journey.

Last Thursday he spent the night sleeping on a pew in a church in Hanson. He said 13-year-old Sean Shanks of one of the church families walked to Plymouth with him Friday morning. "He wanted to walk just eight miles but decided to keep going. His mother gave him the option of going to a fair, but he said he liked the challenge of the long walk," Sweetgall said.

"He ended up walking 32 miles, all the way to Wareham."

Saturday he walked Route 6 from Wareham to New Bedford and Fall River. With motels again full, he slept "on an old wooden bench under a broken pistachio nut machine and the public pay telephone in the police station lobby. The Fall River police were very nice. They brought out blankets and told me to keep my waist pack and possessions close to my body while I slept."

Sunday he walked in the drizzle to Providence "which ought to win an award for the most confusing highway system." Monday he got lost, spending an extra 10 miles walking around Warwick, and finishing the day in Woonsocket.

Sweetgall said that since leaving Woodsocket yesterday morning he has been greeted by many people who have followed his story in The Evening Gazette. As he talked from a telephone booth on Route 20 yesterday morning, drivers honked horns and waved to him.

In Uxbridge, he stopped at Kip's Diner for tomato Florentine soup, cranberry muffins and homemade carrot cake. "It's a real home-cooking kind of restaurant," he said. "That's my kind of place."

Tomorrow he will undergo tests at UMass. Saturday morning he will resume the walk from Sturbridge. Later Saturday he will be taken to UMass, Amherst, for further tests.

During the next week he will be in Connecticut, walking through Hartford, New Haven, Bridgeport, Westport, Norwalk, Stamford and Greenwich to Highway 1 and the Old Post Road to New York.

On Thursday he will walk over the Brooklyn Bridge to South Street Seaport and the finish of the walk.

His loose change collection was $174.19 as of yesterday.

*Aug. 29, 1985* ———————————— *Week 51*

NEW YORK — Robert J. Sweetgall walked over the Brooklyn Bridge into lower Manhattan this morning, ending his year-long walk to publicize the importance of cardiac health and walking.

The walk began 11,208 miles and 363 days ago in Newark, Del., where Sweetgall lives. Joining Sweetgall in today's walk were more than 100 children from the Anna P. Mote School in Newark. Children from the school also joined him on his kickoff walk almost a year ago.

It was fitting that children joined him, Sweetgall said, because his message of health and fitness has been aimed primarily at children.

"It still hasn't hit me that the walk is ending," Sweetgall said yesterday as he approached New York. "I feel a lot of pressure, stress to make the schedule, but it hasn't hit me that this is it."

Sweetgall has walked 208 miles in the past five days. After undergoing testing at the University of Massachusetts Medical Center last Friday, he resumed walking at Sturbridge on Saturday morning.

As with most of his walk in the Worcester area, he wasn't alone. When he started that final leg at 5:45 a.m., he was joined by Joe Vaccariello, 13, of Putnam, Conn., Jane Faucher of Worcester, business manager at WNEB radio; Dotty Leboeuf of Auburn, an elementary school teacher, and this reporter.

Vaccariello, who said he had followed Sweetgall's walk throughout the year and had present-

102

ed weekly updates to his class at the Putnam Middle School, walked 10 miles to Brimfield. He was the first of the walkers to find change along the road, uncovering a penny in the dirt.

As Sweetgall walked through Sturbridge and into Brimfield, drivers honked and some people stopped to walk a short distance with him.

Audrey Farraher of Worcester, a student at Quinsigamond Community College, joined the walk in Brimfield. Ms. Faucher, Ms. Leboeuf, Ms. Farraher and this reporter walked with Sweetgall into Stafford, Conn., the 50th state of the year-long walk.

Sweetgall walked a total of 38 miles Saturday, stopping outside Ellington, Conn., where he got a ride to Amherst for more testing at the University of Massachusetts. He returned to Ellington about 12:30 a.m., Sunday, and resumed walking.

"I knew that to make New York on schedule I would have to walk through the night once in the walk," Sweetgall said. "I decided I might as well do it Saturday night. It was the first time on the trip that I have walked all night."

Sweetgall added 43 miles on Sunday, walking to Wallingford, Conn. Monday he walked through New Haven to Bridgeport. After getting lost for 2½ hours in Bridgeport Tuesday he walked into Stamford.

"Route 1 in Connecticut has been just like being back on Flatbush Avenue in Brooklyn, store after store after store. A lot of dirt and grit and fumes from the trucks and cars going real fast," he said. "I should feel at home, but I don't. I'm so used to being in the country.

"Darien was a nice-looking town. The bricks there seemed real, but Westport seemed really artificial, stores selling cutesy furs, jewelry, leisure shops. I think it must be the Izod alligator capital of the world.

Sweetgall said that as of yesterday morning, his loose change collection was $182.82, an average of 50 cents a day over the past 363 days.

*Sept. 5, 1985 ——————————— Week 52*

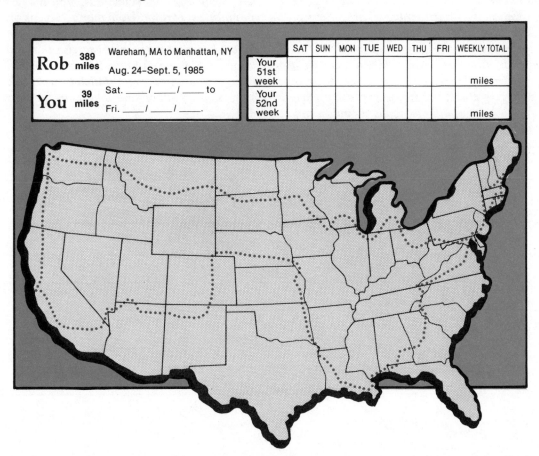

| | | SAT | SUN | MON | TUE | WED | THU | FRI | WEEKLY TOTAL |
|---|---|---|---|---|---|---|---|---|---|
| **Rob** 389 miles | Wareham, MA to Manhattan, NY — Aug. 24–Sept. 5, 1985 | | | | | | | | |
| **You** 39 miles | Sat. ___/___/___ to — Fri. ___/___/___. | | | | | | | | |
| Your 51st week | | | | | | | | | miles |
| Your 52nd week | | | | | | | | | miles |

# Foot Notes     Weeks 51 & 52

---

**51**   **Some Ending Philosophy** ─────────────────

*None of us need be great athletes to walk for wellness. You, me, everyone—we can all walk across America and discover the beauty that lies right in our own backyards. It's there waiting. Yet in our trendy way, we have turned "fitness" into a big business—fancy health clubs and all that shiny chrome. Yet you can get fit walking in fresh air, for free.*

*The jogging boom of the '70's inspired some, but did little for the many who needed inspiration the most. It gave all of us "lounge lizards" the perfect excuse not to exercise. Why pound your body into destruction? Is it worth it? Is it enjoyable? Did you ever see a jogger smile? For 10 years I got caught up in the jogging craze; my fitness perspective became so narrow—like how fast I could run a marathon.*

*More important than short-term fitness is long-term wellness. We've been brainwashed about body weight, body fat, and body muscle. Health clubs are full of muscle-building equipment. Yet did you know anyone who died from "lack of strength?" So many people exercise for all the wrong reasons. To be fit is good, but it's only a temporary state. A week of bad habits, and your fitness is gone. Wellness is lifelong. To achieve it, you make a commitment for life. How many 75-year old weightlifters and aerobic dancers do you know? Walking is the one exercise that will last you a lifetime. And to all those who complain, "Walking takes too much time," I ask, "What's your hurry, and where are you going?"*

---

**52**   👣 **Your Personal Foot Notes** 👣

<br>
<br>
<br>
<br>
<br>
<br>
<br>

104

# Epilogue

**The Corn Fields Never End**   The journey is over, and I face long days of writing in the office. Come evening, when the sun is low and peeking through the venetian blinds, I know it's time to hit the backroads again—to walk along those same corn fields where it all began. The sun setting, spreads pinks and lavenders across the Maryland horizon. Telephone poles and corn stalks become silhouettes. And I dream of walking west again, free and wild, in the cool night air.

For the journeyman having lived a year as a highway road hog, it's a strange feeling waking up that first morning after—realizing there's no town to walk to, no pancakes on the horizon, no children waiting on the edge of town to walk me into school.

No question—I miss the journey. Big question—will I do another? I would really love to, but it's not all that simple. There is my loving mother who wishes not to see her only child come face to face with rolling 60 mph semis. I promised her that this 50-stater would be my last. Then again I made that promise to her at the end of my first journey. Her goal is to see me finally married. Maybe the third walk could kick off with my wedding ceremony—then a long road honeymoon.

It is interesting to see the response I get from audiences I speak to when I ask: "If I did another walk of America, how many of you would like to do it also?" In school presentations about 75% of all children raise their hands—in adult groups, typically 10% to 25%.

The tough question I keep debating is: "Where should I best spend my energies as a walking-for-wellness promoter?" There are so many possibilities: children, corporate employees, seniors, etc. My philosophy is simple; I try not to turn down any group willing to promote walking.

But school children are still my favorite audience. They are the future health of this country. Having visited over 400 school districts since 1981, I am disturbed with our overall state of wellness education. Some states like Oregon are the exception, but most are back in the dark ages of 1940's physical education, emphasizing competitive sports. Take a few good athletes and go for that winning season; leave the majority on the sidelines to cheer. Couple that with our great desire to test children's fitness. How fast can Johnny run a mile? Test after test, Johnny fails. When are we going to stop testing Johnny, and start teaching him some sound principles of aerobics and cardiovascular health? Personally I don't care if "x" percent of our students are overweight and unable to run a mile— as long as they show signs of self-improvement. The latter is what counts.

Since the trek completed, much of my energies have been directed at designing a new walking curriculum—*Walking Wellness*—just for elementary and middle school children. In this course, children are taught *health* and *physical education* with *reading, writing, math* and *lifestyle planning* in 20 creative walking workshops that have teachers and children walking together.

My gut reaction is that if every student in America would walk a mile a day with his or her teacher or parent, most of our drug, disciplinary and learning problems would dissolve away. So now my goal is to motivate educators towards such a way of life. And if I feel that another Robert Sweetgall walk helps accomplish that end—I'll probably do it.

Photo by Joanne Witek.

**Children Love Walking**   At the Fort River Elementary School children learn that walking is entertaining, educational, and exercise. Based on pilot demonstrations at the nationally acclaimed Oaklea Middle School (Junction City, OR), Fort River Elementary will be one of the first schools in the East to teach Walking Wellness as an integrated curriculum.

106

# Appendix

**The End**   In one more footstep an 11,208 mile journey ends. Pier 16, Manhattan, September 5, 1985.

# Journeyman Jargon

**BONKING:** A sharp drop in blood sugar impairing brain function and coordination. Remedy: eat some carbohydrates!

**CADENCE:** The number of right and left footsteps taken per minute. Typical range: 100 to 130.

**CALLUS:** A build-up of dead, thickened, dry skin occurring at pressure points where there is excessive rubbing and friction.

**CHINOOK:** A westerly air movement (upwards of 100 mph) often originating off the eastern slopes of the Rockies.

**CROSS-GRADE:** The side slope of a highway or shoulder measured as percent grade. The steeper the cross-grade, the more stress on the ankles.

**CRUISING:** Walking at the pace that produces essentially no fatigue (typically 3½ mph for many walkers).

**DEHYDRATION:** Excessive loss of body fluid leading to dizziness, fainting or possibly death.

**EIGHT-COLOR MEAL:** A vegetable plate containing 8 different colors of food.

**FOOT RATING:** A score ranging from "0" to "10" characterizing the condition of each foot: "0" hell . . . "4" barely tolerable . . . "8" minor irritation . . . "10" heaven.

**FRIENDLY FACTOR:** Index of how motorists respond to a walker's hand wave.

**HEEL-TOE WALKING:** The walker's natural foot motion: foot strikes on the heel, rolls over the ball and pushes off on the toes.

**HYPOTHERMIA:** Excessive drop in body temperature due to rapid heat loss.

**ORTHOTICS:** Corrective devices that when placed under the foot, inside the shoe, align the leg properly in true vertical position.

**PRONATION:** An excessive inward rotation of the foot on landing, more typical of people with flat feet.

**SIDE STITCHES:** Sharp, shooting pains in the abdominal area—often caused by insufficient warm-up or trapped gas after a meal.

**SIX-CALENDAR CAFE:** A ma & pa restaurant that serves real, home-cooked meals at reasonable prices (termed by Wm. Least Heat Moon, Blue Highways)

**STRIDE LENGTH:** The consistent distance measured between 2 consecutive footsteps—left heel strike to right heel strike.

**TRAFFIC DENSITY:** The number of cars passing a given point per hour on the highway. Normal: 500 to 1,000 per hour—busy: 5,000 to 10,000 per hour.

**THE WHITE LINE:** The 4" wide stripe of white paint separating the shoulder from the right lane of traffic—often the levelest portion of the highway to walk on.

**WIND CHILL FACTOR:** A measure of the combined effect of wind and temperature on body heat loss.

# The Best and Worst of Walking America

On a yearlong walk you see it all—from Joshua trees hanging in the fiery orange sunset, to refinery flares flicking their yellow fingers in the smog. When you marry a journey, you must live with all her personalities, for better or worse, as you will see below.

**Cleanest Town on Tour:** Mt. Horeb, WI.  **Dirtiest Town:** NYC  **Cleanest State:** Oregon  **Prettiest, Cleanest Major City:** Portland, OR  **Best Air Quality:** Eastern Montana, Central Washington  **Poorest Air Quality:** Missoula, MT (Woodsmoke and pulp plant emissions), Northeast N.J. (Chemicals), Gothenberg, NE (Alfalfa/Hay dust)

**Most Hazardous Highway:** New Jersey's traffic circles  **Worst Marked Roads:** New England (as a region)  **Worst Highway Shoulders:** Taos, NM (slick, red mud)  **Worst Road Surface:** Pearlblossom, CA to Victorville, CA (Mojave Desert) and New Boston, TX to Texarkana  **Most Scenic Country:** Zion National Park, UT and Echo Cliffs, AZ  **Longest Monotonous Stretch:** Nebraska Highway 30 (250 miles)

**Friendliest Folks:** Louisiana, North Dakota  **Warmest Citizen Response:** Worcester, MA and Shreveport, LA  **Most Locked Doors and Security Barriers:** Southern California (Santa Barbara, Mojave Desert)  **Most Aggressive Drivers:** Texarkana (Texas side) and Highway 123 west of Clemson, S.C.  **Most Unforgetable Person:** Maurey "Steam Train" Graham (King of the Hoboes)

**Most Popular Highway Kill:** The Texas Armadillo  **Most Interesting Wildlife:** Montana (elk, deer, antelope, coyote, wild turkey) and New York City (humans)

**Most Helpful Police:** Montana Highway Patrol  **Nicest Jail Cell Accomodations:** Pascagoula, MS  **Best Lodging Buy:** American Youth Hostel (Ashland, OR).  **Most Ride Offers in a Day:** Bozeman Pass, Montana

**Best Stretch for Finding Coins:** Route 1 from Portland, ME to Boston, MA  **Tightest Loose Change States:** W. Virginia, Alaska, Texas, The Dakotas  **Most Reasonable Cafes:** Iowa  **Most Expensive Food:** Alaska  **Best Breakfast Buy:** The Slot Joint, Las Vegas (79¢ for unlimited pancakes)  **Best Breakfast:** Linda's French Toast on the "Slash J" Ranch  **Best Dinner:** Pepino's (pasta) in Ashland, OR

**Toughest Terrain:** Appalachian Mountains west of Hancock, MD  **Toughest Weather:** Hettinger, ND (60 mph freezing headwinds for 26 miles) and Coulee City, WA (−30° wind chill, 31 miles)  **Worst Airborne Insects:** New Orleans, LA to Biloxi, MS (black flies, mosquitos, nats).  **Worst Ground Insects:** fire ants (30 bites on one arm north of Mobile)

**Best Media Coverage:** The Evening Gazette.

**Leading State for Wellness Education:** Oregon

# Ten Walking Tips

**1** **The Principle of Recovery**

As Edward Payson Weston advised—after any walking performance, you should always be able to come back the very next day and repeat it. Weston himself often walked 50 miles a day, day after day.

**2** **When to Walk**

Walk anytime! If you walk after meals, slow down enough to give digestion a chance. No time is better than the time that suits you. Regularity is the key factor.

**3** **Natural Gaited Walking**

The best walking technique is the one that's natural for you. Walking with weights (ankle weights or hand weights) is unnatural. Weights change your center of gravity, rhythm and bio-mechanics, not to mention the ballistic stress they put on your connective tissues.

**4** **3½ MPH Walking**

3½ mph walking is about the most important speed a walker can learn. This pace causes little fatigue or leg soreness. It's your all-family, stay-together pace. Yet 3½ mph is not all that slow. At 3½ mph, stored fat becomes the major source of fuel for your working muscles.

**5** **Hills**

In climbing, lean forward into the hill. Do not hesitate to slow up your pace. In descending, shift your weight back, taking shorter shuffle steps.

**6** **Warming Up & Cooling Down**

Walking is the best warm-up/cool-down exercise because it doesn't strain cold muscles, and it helps the heart and blood vessels adjust gradually to blood circulation changes. If you are a 4 mph walker for example, consider warming-up (and cooling down) at 3½ mph.

**7** **Daytime Foot Care**

"Listen" to your feet talk. When they start whispering "We're getting warm," that's the time to slip off your shoes. Immediately! Then air cool, clean and re-powder your feet.

**8** **Nighttime Foot Care**

Avoid hard cracky callus skin by soaking and washing your feet in warm water. After drying, message in wool's fat (lanolin) on all foot surfaces (assuming no allergy to lanolin). Sleep with your feet in open air for good oxygen exchange.

**9** **Mind Games**

When boredom starts to set in, change the subject! Think of dinner. Observe the clouds. Plan a family outing. Start looking for loose change. If your mind is occupied, it's hard to get bored.

**10** **Walking Off Weight**

The best way to walk off weight is to walk for time. Sitting down right now you are burning about 1 calorie per minute. When you stand up and start walking, your metabolic rate increases to about 5 calories per minute.

# The Walking Calories Chart[†]

| Food Item | Total Calories | Minutes Of Walking To Burn Up Calories |
|---|---|---|
| water | 0 | |
| 12 oz. club soda | 1 | |
| 1 cup lettuce | 10 | |
| 1 cup raw spinach | 15 | |
| sm. cucumber | 25 | |
| 1 cup string beans | 30 | |
| 1 cup watermelon | 40 | |
| 1 cup popcorn | 40 | |
| ½ canteloupe | 50 | |
| 1 oatmeal cookie | 50 | |
| 1 tbs maple syrup | 50* | |
| slice bread | 65 | |
| 1 orange | 75 | |
| 1 cup grapes | 75 | |
| 1 tbs peanut butter | 95 | |
| 1 fried egg | 100 | |
| med. banana | 100 | |
| slice American cheese | 105 | |
| 1 cup orange juice | 115 | |
| 1 cup apple juice | 115 | |
| 1 cup cooked peas | 115 | |
| slice buttered bread | 125 | |
| 1 cup hot oatmeal | 130 | |
| 12 oz. cola | 150* | |
| 1 cup wild rice | 150 | |
| 1 cup whole milk | 160 | |
| med. baked potato (plain) | 170 | |
| 12 oz. beer* | 180 | |
| ½ cup raisins | 210 | |
| slice pizza* | 225 | |
| 1 cup ice cream* | 250 | |
| slice apple pie* | 250 | |
| 1 choc. candy bar* | 250 | |
| lg. french fries* | 300 | |
| med. fast food burger* | 360 | |
| 2 pc. crispy fried chicken* | 500 | |
| 1 fast food fried fish sand.* | 500 | |
| 1 slice pie ala mode* | 500 | |
| 1 extra thick shake* | 700 | |

Scale (Minutes Of Walking To Burn Up Calories): 0  15  30  45  60  75  90  105  120  140

*Poor diet choice due to either high sugar, high salt (sodium), high fat or alcohol content.

†Caloric values based primarily on USDA Agricultural Handbook Data and American Council on Science & Health Data.

# Nights On The Road

Shown below are the towns where Rob wound up spending his 364 nights. As you log your progress across America (page 115), you can compare your adjusted mileage totals to Rob's to figure out where you'd be sleeping, come each Friday night.

| DAY | DAY # | STATE | DESTINATION | CUMUL. MILES |
|-----|-------|-------|-------------|--------------|
| FRI | ½ | MD | Northeast | 18 |
| SAT | 1 | MD | Bel Air | 47 |
| SUN | 2 | MD | Hamstead | 80 |
| MON | 3 | MD | Graceham | 114 |
| TUE | 4 | MD | Clear Spring | 152 |
| WED | 5 | MD | Hancock | 177 |
| THU | 6 | MD | Breakneck Hill | 210 |
| FRI | 7 | MD | Frostburg | 232 |
| SAT | 8 | PA | Markleysburg | 266 |
| SUN | 9 | PA | Brownsville | 297 |
| MON | 10 | PA | Washington | 321 |
| TUE | 11 | PA | Claysville | 342 |
| WED | 12 | OH | St. Clairsville | 375 |
| THU | 13 | OH | Cambridge | 413 |
| FRI | 14 | OH | Zanesville | 448 |
| SAT | 15 | OH | Reynoldsburg | 488 |
| SUN | 16 | OH | Delaware | 522 |
| MON | 17 | OH | Marion | 547 |
| TUE | 18 | OH | Carey | 580 |
| WED | 19 | OH | New Rochester | 604 |
| THU | 20 | OH | Maumee | 631 |
| FRI | 21 | MI | Ida | 655 |
| SAT | 22 | OH | (Toledo) | 678 |
| SUN | 23 | MI | Maybee | 694 |
| MON | 24 | MI | Novi | 732 |
| TUE | 25 | MI | Howell | 759 |
| WED | 26 | MI | Perry | 792 |
| THU | 27 | MI | Potterville | 825 |
| FRI | 28 | MI | Battle Creek | 863 |
| SAT | 29 | MI | Schoolcraft | 900 |
| SUN | 30 | MI | Cassopolis | 933 |
| MON | 31 | IN | South Bend | 960 |
| TUE | 32 | IN | Town of Pines | 998 |
| WED | 33 | IL | S. Chicago | 1035 |
| THU | 34 | MA | (Worcester) | 1050 |
| FRI | 35 | MA | (Worcester) | 1060 |
| SAT | 36 | MA | (Boston) | 1066 |
| SUN | 37 | IL | Park Ridge | 1096 |
| MON | 38 | IL | Crystal Lake | 1129 |
| TUE | 39 | WI | Darien | 1170 |
| WED | 40 | WI | Brooklyn | 1211 |
| THU | 41 | WI | Mt. Horeb | 1238 |
| FRI | 42 | WI | Mineral Point | 1268 |
| SAT | 43 | IA | Dubuque | 1311 |
| SUN | 44 | IA | Millville | 1344 |
| MON | 45 | IA | Garnavillo | 1362 |
| TUE | 46 | IA | Decorah | 1411 |
| WED | 47 | MN | Preston | 1449 |
| THU | 48 | MN | Rochester | 1485 |
| FRI | 49 | MN | Hader | 1525 |
| SAT | 50 | MN | Pine Island | 1554 |
| SUN | 51 | MN | Minneapolis | 1592 |
| MON | 52 | MN | St. Louis Park | 1601 |
| TUE | 53 | MN | Howard Lake | 1632 |
| WED | 54 | MN | Litchfield | 1656 |
| THU | 55 | MN | Willmar | 1688 |
| FRI | 56 | MN | Benson | 1718 |
| SAT | 57 | MN | E. Ortonville | 1748 |
| SUN | 58 | SD | Milbank | 1779 |
| MON | 59 | SD | Waubay | 1817 |
| TUE | 60 | SD | Groton | 1858 |
| WED | 61 | SD | Aberdeen | 1881 |
| THU | 62 | SD | Roscoe | 1924 |
| FRI | 63 | SD | Java | 1956 |
| SAT | 64 | SD | Mobridge | 1987 |
| SUN | 65 | SD | McLaughlin | 2019 |
| MON | 66 | SD | Watauga | 2056 |
| TUE | 67 | SD | White Butte | 2091 |
| WED | 68 | ND | Bucyrus | 2116 |
| THU | 69 | ND | Buffalo Springs | 2145 |
| FRI | 70 | ND | Marmarth | 2181 |
| SAT | 71 | MT | Plevna | 2222 |
| SUN | 72 | MT | Locate | 2254 |
| MON | 73 | MT | Miles City | 2285 |
| TUE | 74 | MT | Rosebud | 2319 |
| WED | 75 | MT | Hysham | 2356 |
| THU | 76 | MT | Custer | 2391 |
| FRI | 77 | MT | Huntley | 2431 |
| SAT | 78 | MA | (Worcester) | 2438 |
| SUN | 79 | MA | (Worcester) | 2443 |
| MON | 80 | MA | (Boston) | 2456 |
| TUE | 81 | MT | W. Billings | 2462 |
| WED | 82 | MT | Columbus | 2501 |
| THU | 83 | MT | Big Timber | 2542 |
| FRI | 84 | MT | Livingston | 2577 |
| SAT | 85 | MT | Belgrade | 2613 |
| SUN | 86 | MT | Toston | 2653 |
| MON | 87 | MT | Winston | 2680 |
| TUE | 88 | MT | Helena | 2707 |
| WED | 89 | MT | Elliston | 2729 |
| THU | 90 | MT | Goldcreek | 2762 |
| FRI | 91 | MT | Rock Creek | 2800 |
| SAT | 92 | MT | E. Missoula | 2832 |
| SUN | 93 | MT | Superior | 2882 |
| MON | 94 | MT | Haugan | 2914 |
| TUE | 95 | ID | Kellog | 2956 |
| WED | 96 | ID | Coeur D'Alene | 2992 |
| THU | 97 | WA | Spokane | 3024 |
| FRI | 98 | WA | Spokane | 3036 |
| SAT | 99 | WA | W. Davenport | 3078 |
| SUN | 100 | WA | Wilbur | 3103 |
| MON | 101 | WA | Coulee City | 3136 |
| TUE | 102 | WA | Ephrata | 3166 |
| WED | 103 | WA | Rock Island | 3204 |
| THU | 104 | WA | Cashmere | 3228 |
| FRI | 105 | WA | Tumwater Canyon | 3263 |

| DAY | DAY # | STATE | DESTINATION | CUMUL. MILES | DAY | DAY # | STATE | DESTINATION | CUMUL. MILES |
|-----|-------|-------|-------------|--------------|-----|-------|-------|-------------|--------------|
| SAT | 106 | WA | Skykomish | 3294 | SAT | 169 | UT | St. George | 5247 |
| SUN | 107 | WA | Monroe | 3330 | SUN | 170 | UT | Rockville | 5282 |
| MON | 108 | WA | Seattle | 3361 | MON | 171 | UT | Mt. Carmel | 5316 |
| TUE | 109 | WA | Tocoma | 3402 | TUE | 172 | UT | Johnson Canyon | 5343 |
| WED | 110 | WA | Olympia | 3428 | WED | 173 | UT | Glen Canyon | 5383 |
| THU | 111 | MA | (Worcester) | 3430 | THU | 174 | AZ | Page | 5411 |
| FRI | 112 | MA | (Worcester) | 3443 | FRI | 175 | AZ | Echo Cliffs | 5447 |
| SAT | 113 | AK | Anchorage | 3444 | SAT | 176 | AZ | The Gap | 5478 |
| SUN | 114 | WA | Seatac Airport | 3455 | SUN | 177 | AZ | Cameron | 5514 |
| MON | 115 | WA | Chehalis | 3489 | MON | 178 | AZ | N. Flagstaff | 5532 |
| TUE | 116 | WA | Castle Rock | 3522 | TUE | 179 | AZ | Winona | 5560 |
| WED | 117 | OR | St. Helens | 3561 | WED | 180 | AZ | Winslow | 5598 |
| THU | 118 | OR | Portland | 3592 | THU | 181 | AZ | Holbrook | 5632 |
| FRI | 119 | OR | Woodburn | 3618 | FRI | 182 | AZ | Navajo | 5659 |
| SAT | 120 | OR | Albany | 3660 | SAT | 183 | AZ | Lupton | 5692 |
| SUN | 121 | OR | Harrisburg | 3692 | SUN | 184 | NM | Gallup | 5730 |
| MON | 122 | OR | Eugene | 3717 | MON | 185 | NM | Continental Divide | 5757 |
| TUE | 123 | OR | Curtin | 3750 | TUE | 186 | NM | Grants | 5794 |
| WED | 124 | OR | Roseburg | 3788 | WED | 187 | NM | Laguna | 5830 |
| THU | 125 | OR | Tri-City | 3812 | THU | 188 | NM | W. Albuquerque | 5867 |
| FRI | 126 | OR | Wolf Creek | 3841 | FRI | 189 | NM | Bernadillo | 5897 |
| SAT | 127 | OR | Gold Hill | 3879 | SAT | 190 | NM | S. Santa Fe | 5934 |
| SUN | 128 | OR | Ashland | 3906 | SUN | 191 | NM | Pojaque | 5961 |
| MON | 129 | CA | Hornbrook | 3939 | MON | 192 | NM | Rinconado | 5991 |
| TUE | 130 | CA | Gazelle | 3969 | TUE | 193 | NM | Taos | 6019 |
| WED | 131 | CA | Dunsmuir | 4000 | WED | 194 | NM | Eagle Nest | 6051 |
| THU | 132 | CA | Lakehead | 4029 | THU | 195 | NM | N. Cimarron | 6088 |
| FRI | 133 | CA | Cottonwood | 4070 | FRI | 196 | NM | (Santa Fe) | 6093 |
| SAT | 134 | CA | Los Molinas | 4104 | SAT | 197 | NM | (Santa Fe) | 6106 |
| SUN | 135 | CA | Durham | 4143 | SUN | 198 | NM | S. Raton | 6146 |
| MON | 136 | CA | Marysville | 4185 | MON | 199 | CO | Trinidad | 6187 |
| TUE | 137 | CA | Knights Landing | 4218 | TUE | 200 | CO | Walsenburg | 6211 |
| WED | 138 | CA | Sacramento | 4245 | WED | 201 | CO | Pueblo | 6242 |
| THU | 139 | CA | Vacaville | 4273 | THU | 202 | CO | Widefield | 6273 |
| FRI | 140 | CA | Vallejo | 4304 | FRI | 203 | CO | N. Colorado Springs | 6294 |
| SAT | 141 | CA | San Rafael | 4342 | SAT | 204 | CO | Castle Rock | 6327 |
| SUN | 142 | CA | San Francisco | 4376 | SUN | 205 | CO | Arvada | 6364 |
| MON | 143 | HI | Honolulu | 4397 | MON | 206 | CO | Longmont | 6396 |
| TUE | 144 | CA | San Mateo | 4413 | TUE | 207 | CO | Loveland | 6424 |
| WED | 145 | CA | Palo Alto | 4424 | WED | 208 | CO | (Worcester) | 6429 |
| THU | 146 | CA | San Jose | 4470 | THU | 209 | CO | (Worcester) | 6440 |
| FRI | 147 | CA | Salinas | 4510 | FRI | 210 | CO | Loveland | 6442 |
| SAT | 148 | CA | Greenfield | 4552 | SAT | 211 | WY | Wellington | 6470 |
| SUN | 149 | CA | San Miguel | 4611 | SUN | 212 | WY | Cheyenne | 6507 |
| MON | 150 | CA | Atascadero | 4635 | MON | 213 | WY | Burne | 6531 |
| TUE | 151 | CA | Santa Maria | 4680 | TUE | 214 | NE | Bushnell | 6565 |
| WED | 152 | CA | Santa Ynez | 4719 | WED | 215 | NE | Potter | 6600 |
| THU | 153 | CA | Carpinteria | 4763 | THU | 216 | NE | Lodgepole | 6635 |
| FRI | 154 | CA | Ventura | 4780 | FRI | 217 | NE | Big Springs | 6668 |
| SAT | 155 | CA | Fillmore | 4807 | SAT | 218 | NE | Paxton | 6708 |
| SUN | 156 | CA | Canyon Country | 4835 | SUN | 219 | NE | North Platte | 6743 |
| MON | 157 | CA | Littlerock | 4870 | MON | 220 | NE | Gothenburg | 6779 |
| TUE | 158 | CA | Victorville | 4902 | TUE | 221 | NE | Lexington | 6808 |
| WED | 159 | CA | Hodge | 4934 | WED | 222 | NE | Odessa | 6843 |
| THU | 160 | CA | Yermo | 4964 | THU | 223 | NE | Wood River | 6876 |
| FRI | 161 | CA | Beacon Station | 5004 | FRI | 224 | NE | Aurora | 6913 |
| SAT | 162 | CA | Valley Wells | 5044 | SAT | 225 | NE | Utica | 6950 |
| SUN | 163 | NV | Jean | 5082 | SUN | 226 | NE | Lincoln | 6987 |
| MON | 164 | NV | S. Las Vegas | 5105 | MON | 227 | NE | Palmyra | 7011 |
| TUE | 165 | MA | (Worcester) | 5116 | TUE | 228 | NE | Nebraska City | 7042 |
| WED | 166 | NV | Las Vegas | 5121 | WED | 229 | NE | Auburn | 7065 |
| THU | 167 | NV | Valley of Fire | 5163 | THU | 230 | MO | Craig | 7101 |
| FRI | 168 | NV | Mesquite | 5206 | FRI | 231 | MO | Nodaway | 7135 |

| DAY | DAY # | STATE | DESTINATION | CUMUL. MILES | DAY | DAY # | STATE | DESTINATION | CUMUL. MILES |
|---|---|---|---|---|---|---|---|---|---|
| SAT | 232 | KS | Atchison | 7179 | SAT | 295 | SC | Seneca | 9068 |
| SUN | 233 | KS | Meriden | 7218 | SUN | 296 | SC | Travelers Rest | 9106 |
| MON | 234 | KS | Perry | 7242 | MON | 297 | NC | Hendersonville | 9135 |
| TUE | 235 | KS | Kansas City | 7275 | TUE | 298 | NC | Weaverville | 9165 |
| WED | 236 | KS | Olathe | 7296 | WED | 299 | TN | Erwin | 9203 |
| THU | 237 | KS | Osawatomie | 7324 | THU | 300 | TN | Kingsport | 9243 |
| FRI | 238 | KS | Garnett | 7352 | FRI | 301 | VA | Duffield | 9280 |
| SAT | 239 | KS | Iola | 7392 | SAT | 302 | VA | Wise | 9315 |
| SUN | 240 | KS | Thayer | 7424 | SUN | 303 | VA | Elkhorn City | 9357 |
| MON | 241 | KS | Coffeyville | 7453 | MON | 304 | VA | Grimsleyville | 9392 |
| TUE | 242 | OK | Nowata | 7478 | TUE | 305 | VA | Maxwell | 9424 |
| WED | 243 | OK | N. Tulsa | 7515 | WED | 306 | VA | Bluefield | 9456 |
| THU | 244 | MA | (Worcester) | 7534 | THU | 307 | VA | Pearisburg | 9496 |
| FRI | 245 | MA | (Worcester) | 7547 | FRI | 308 | VA | Christianburg | 9534 |
| SAT | 246 | MA | (Worcester) | 7549 | SAT | 309 | VA | Roanoke | 9567 |
| SUN | 247 | OK | Bixby | 7564 | SUN | 310 | VA | Forest | 9608 |
| MON | 248 | OK | Haskell | 7584 | MON | 311 | VA | Amherst | 9634 |
| TUE | 249 | OK | Warner | 7624 | TUE | 312 | VA | Myndus | 9666 |
| WED | 250 | OK | Sallisaw | 7659 | WED | 313 | MA | (Worcester) | 9695 |
| THU | 251 | OK | Poteau | 7693 | THU | 314 | MA | (Worcester) | 9707 |
| FRI | 252 | OK | Zoe | 7724 | FRI | 315 | MA | Madison | 9734 |
| SAT | 253 | AR | Mena | 7756 | SAT | 316 | VA | Remington | 9766 |
| SUN | 254 | AR | De Queen | 7801 | SUN | 317 | VA | Fairfax | 9805 |
| MON | 255 | AR | Foreman | 7831 | MON | 318 | MD | College Park | 9834 |
| TUE | 256 | TX | Texarkana | 7867 | TUE | 319 | MD | Baltimore | 9867 |
| WED | 257 | AR | Fouke | 7889 | WED | 320 | MD | Havre De Grace | 9903 |
| THU | 258 | LA | Hosston | 7918 | THU | 321 | DE | Newark | 9925 |
| FRI | 259 | LA | N. Shreveport | 7938 | FRI | 322 | DE | Newark | 9951 |
| SAT | 260 | LA | Loggy Bayou | 7979 | SAT | 323 | DE | Wilmington | 9974 |
| SUN | 261 | LA | Campti | 8015 | SUN | 324 | PA | Philadelphia | 10012 |
| MON | 262 | LA | Colfax | 8051 | MON | 325 | NJ | Willingboro | 10041 |
| TUE | 263 | LA | Alexandria | 8080 | TUE | 326 | NJ | Princeton | 10078 |
| WED | 264 | LA | Marksville | 8107 | WED | 327 | NJ | Edison | 10108 |
| THU | 265 | LA | Simmesport | 8134 | THU | 328 | NJ | Westfield | 10138 |
| FRI | 266 | LA | New Roads | 8168 | FRI | 329 | NJ | Passaic | 10172 |
| SAT | 267 | LA | Baton Rouge | 8201 | SAT | 330 | NY | Sloatsburg | 10205 |
| SUN | 268 | LA | Sorrento | 8232 | SUN | 331 | NY | Central Valley | 10231 |
| MON | 269 | LA | Reserve | 8268 | MON | 332 | NY | Highland | 10260 |
| TUE | 270 | LA | New Orleans | 8301 | TUE | 333 | NY | Saugerties | 10292 |
| WED | 271 | LA | Michoud | 8322 | WED | 334 | NY | Ravena | 10324 |
| THU | 272 | MS | Pearlington | 8352 | THU | 335 | NY | Hoosick | 10360 |
| FRI | 273 | MS | Pass Christian | 8383 | FRI | 336 | VT | Woodford | 10392 |
| SAT | 274 | MS | Pascagoula | 8421 | SAT | 337 | VT | Brattleboro | 10426 |
| SUN | 275 | AL | Theodore | 8454 | SUN | 338 | NH | Peterborough | 10466 |
| MON | 276 | AL | Saraland | 8478 | MON | 339 | NH | Manchester | 10505 |
| TUE | 277 | AL | Bay Minette | 8508 | TUE | 340 | NH | Northwood | 10535 |
| WED | 278 | AL | Atmore | 8533 | WED | 341 | ME | N. Berwick | 10565 |
| THU | 279 | AL | Brewton | 8566 | THU | 342 | ME | S. Portland | 10601 |
| FRI | 280 | AL | Evergreen | 8599 | FRI | 343 | ME | Saco | 10630 |
| SAT | 281 | AL | Greenville | 8636 | SAT | 344 | NH | Portsmouth | 10667 |
| SUN | 282 | AL | Montgomery | 8680 | SUN | 345 | MA | Rowley | 10702 |
| MON | 283 | AL | Wetumpka | 8707 | MON | 346 | MA | Danvers | 10713 |
| TUE | 284 | AL | Alexander City | 8746 | TUE | 347 | MA | Charlestown | 10736 |
| WED | 285 | AL | Wadley | 8781 | WED | 348 | MA | Canton | 10761 |
| THU | 286 | GA | Franklin | 8814 | THU | 349 | MA | S. Hanson | 10787 |
| FRI | 287 | GA | Carrollton | 8849 | FRI | 350 | MA | Wareham | 10819 |
| SAT | 288 | GA | N. Atlanta | 8882 | SAT | 351 | MA | Fall River | 10854 |
| SUN | 289 | GA | Marietta | 8913 | SUN | 352 | RI | Warwick | 10887 |
| MON | 290 | GA | Marietta | 8920 | MON | 353 | RI | Woonsocket | 10924 |
| TUE | 291 | GA | Alpharetta | 8942 | TUE | 354 | MA | Auburn | 10957 |
| WED | 292 | GA | Cumming | 8966 | WED | 355 | MA | Northboro | 10984 |
| THU | 293 | GA | Lula | 8997 | THU | 356 | MA | Sturbridge | 11009 |
| FRI | 294 | GA | Toccoa | 9028 | FRI | 357 | MA | (Worcester) | 11025 |
|  |  |  |  |  | SAT | 358 | CT | Ellington | 11063 |
|  |  |  |  |  | SUN | 359 | CT | Wallingsford | 11102 |
|  |  |  |  |  | MON | 360 | CT | Bridgeport | 11134 |
|  |  |  |  |  | TUE | 361 | CT | Darien | 11166 |
|  |  |  |  |  | WED | 362 | NY | Manhattan | 11205 |
|  |  |  |  |  | THU | 363 | NY | Manhattan | 11208 |

# Your Walk—America Mileage Log

**To walk your way across America:**

1. Enter your 2-week mileage total.
2. Enter your total up-to-date (cumulative) mileage.
3. Multiply column C by 10, and enter your adjusted mileage.

4. After checking pages 112–114, enter your Friday night field position to see if you're on pace for walking 50-states in a year with Rob.

| A | B | C | D | E | F | G | |
|---|---|---|---|---|---|---|---|
| **Weeks** | Your 2-Week Mileage | Your Cumulative Mileage | | Your Adjusted Mileage | Rob's Cumulative Mileage | Rob's Friday Stopping point | Your Friday Night field position |
| 1 & 2 | | | × 10 = | ↔ | 448 | Zanesville, OH | ↔ |
| 3 & 4 | | | × 10 = | ↔ | 863 | Battlecreek, MI | ↔ |
| 5 & 6 | | | × 10 = | ↔ | 1,268 | Mineral Point, WI | ↔ |
| 7 & 8 | | | × 10 = | ↔ | 1,718 | Benson, MN | ↔ |
| 9 & 10 | | | × 10 = | ↔ | 2,181 | Marmarth, ND | ↔ |
| 11 & 12 | | | × 10 = | ↔ | 2,577 | Livingston, MT | ↔ |
| 13 & 14 | | | × 10 = | ↔ | 3,036 | Spokane, WA | ↔ |
| 15 & 16 | | | × 10 = | ↔ | 3,443 | Olympia, WA | ↔ |
| 17 & 18 | | | × 10 = | ↔ | 3,841 | Wolf Creek, OR | ↔ |
| 19 & 20 | | | × 10 = | ↔ | 4,304 | Vallejo, CA | ↔ |
| 21 & 22 | | | × 10 = | ↔ | 4,780 | Ventura, CA | ↔ |
| 23 & 24 | | | × 10 = | ↔ | 5,206 | Mesquite, NV | ↔ |
| 25 & 26 | | | × 10 = | ↔ | 5,659 | Navajo, AZ | ↔ |
| 27 & 28 | | | × 10 = | ↔ | 6,093 | N. Cimarron, NM | ↔ |
| 29 & 30 | | | × 10 = | ↔ | 6,442 | Loveland, CO | ↔ |
| 31 & 32 | | | × 10 = | ↔ | 6,913 | Aurora, NE | ↔ |
| 33 & 34 | | | × 10 = | ↔ | 7,352 | Garnett, KS | ↔ |
| 35 & 36 | | | × 10 = | ↔ | 7,724 | Zoe, OK | ↔ |
| 37 & 38 | | | × 10 = | ↔ | 8,168 | New Roads, LA | ↔ |
| 39 & 40 | | | × 10 = | ↔ | 8,599 | Evergreen, AL | ↔ |
| 41 & 42 | | | × 10 = | ↔ | 9,028 | Toccoa, GA | ↔ |
| 43 & 44 | | | × 10 = | ↔ | 9,534 | Christianburg, VA | ↔ |
| 45 & 46 | | | × 10 = | ↔ | 9,951 | Newark, DE | ↔ |
| 47 & 48 | | | × 10 = | ↔ | 10,392 | Woodford, VT | ↔ |
| 49 & 50 | | | × 10 = | ↔ | 10,819 | Wareham, MA | ↔ |
| 51 & 52 | | | × 10 = | ↔ | 11,208 | Manhattan, N.Y. | ↔ |

# The Authors

**Robert Sweetgall** is a serious pedestrian who loves to walk and talk in all kinds of places. Occasionally he pulls off the highway to write a book and conduct motivational walking—wellness workshops for children and adults.

**John Dignam** is the health/science writer for The (Worcester, MA) Evening Gazette. Occasionally he gets an assignment that takes him out on the road for a walk—90 miles worth in Sweetgall's case.

Photo by John Lusk.

**Robert Sweetgall and John Dignam** minutes before setting out to cross the Brooklyn Bridge in the final 2 miles of the long walk.